This book belongs to

_____

...*a woman after God's own heart.*

RELYING
ON THE
POWER OF
THE SPIRIT

ELIZABETH
GEORGE

HARVEST HOUSE PUBLISHERS
EUGENE, OREGON

Cover by Dugan Design Group, Bloomington, Minnesota

Cover photos © frenta / Fotolia; Jihan Abdalla / Getty

Harvest House Publishers, Inc. is the exclusive licensee of the trademark A WOMAN AFTER GOD'S OWN HEART.

Acknowledgments

As always, thank you to my dear husband, Jim George, M.Div., Th.M., for your able assistance, guidance, suggestions, and loving encouragement on this project.

Contents

Before You Begin

*I*n my book *A Woman After God's Own Heart*®, I describe such a woman as one who ensures that God is first in her heart and the Ultimate Priority of her life. Then I share that one crucial way this desire can become reality is by nurturing a heart that abides in God's Word. To do so means that you and I must develop a root system anchored deep in God's Word.

Before you launch into this Bible study, take a moment to think about these aspects of a root system produced by the regular, faithful study of God's Word:

- *Roots are unseen*—You'll want to set aside time in solitude—"underground" if you will—to immerse yourself in God's Word and grow in Him.

- *Roots are for taking in*—Alone and with your Bible in hand, you'll want to take in and feed upon the truths of the Word of God and ensure your spiritual growth.

- *Roots are for storage*—As you form the habit of looking into God's Word, you'll find a vast, deep reservoir of divine hope and strength forming for the rough times.

- *Roots are for support*—Do you want to stand strong in the Lord? To stand firm against the pressures of life? The routine care of your roots through exposure to God's Word will cultivate you into a remarkable woman of endurance.[1]

I'm glad you've chosen this study out of my A Woman After God's Own Heart® Bible study series. My prayer for you is that the truths you find in God's Word through this study will further transform your life into the image of His dear Son and empower you to be the woman you seek to be: a woman after God's own heart.

In His love,

Elizabeth George

Waiting for the Promise

ACTS 1

As you journey through the book of Acts, you will follow the thrilling progress of the birth of the church and its spread throughout the regions bordering the Mediterranean Sea over a 30-year time span.

In reality the book of Acts could be entitled "The Acts of the Holy Spirit." This book of the Bible could be seen as volume 2 in the ongoing story of the life and ministry of Jesus. What Jesus began in the Gospel of Luke in a *limited* physical body, He continues in Acts through the *unlimited* power of His Spirit working in and through His followers.

But in truth, the activities of the book of Acts have never ended. It's a story of what Jesus "began to do and teach" (Acts 1:1). Now, over 2000 years later, you are asked to continue the work that Jesus and the early church began. The baton has been passed on to you. Relying on the power of the Holy Spirit, you too are asked to pass on to others what Jesus began.

God's Message...

1. Read Luke 1:1-4. Who wrote this Gospel, and what was his purpose?

2. Read Acts 1:1-5 and answer the following questions:

   Compare Acts 1:1 with Luke 1:1-4. What additional information do you receive from this second book written by Luke?

   What did the risen Savior "do" (verse 3)?

   What did He teach (verse 3)?

   What twofold command did He give (verses 4-5)?
   —

   —

3. Read Acts 1:6-11 and the disciples' concerns in verse 6.

   What answer did the Lord give them (verse 7)?

Describe the geographical progression that the gospel message would take (verse 8).

Where would the power come from for this worldwide mission?

Briefly describe the events of verses 9-11. (Theologians refer to what happened in these verses as "the ascension.")

4. Now read Acts 1:12-14 and list the three groups of people who responded to the instructions of "the men in white."

    —

    —

    —

   What were they doing?

5. Read 1:15-25 and briefly describe what takes place.

... and Your Heart's Response

- *Base your faith on facts.* Christians are often accused of foolishly taking a giant leap of faith in the dark. Luke, however, gives just the opposite view. He points to the verifiable fact that Jesus appeared to hundreds of people over a period of 40 days after His resurrection. Armed with the reality of His resurrection, His faithful followers went out and boldly preached Jesus to the world. How should knowing that your faith is supported by solid historical facts help you as a witness for Jesus?

- *Know your Bible.* As you look again at Peter's speech in the upper room (Acts 1:15-25), he quotes numerous verses from the Old Testament. His thoughts and speech centered on his knowledge of the truths of Scripture. What are you doing to deepen your knowledge of Scripture? What difference should this make in your daily life and actions?

Relying on the Power of the Spirit

If you are a believer in Jesus Christ, you are part of a rich heritage that started at the beginning of recorded history in the Garden of Eden. When all seemed to be lost, God promised to send someone who would defeat Satan. The Old

Testament predicted the coming of this Savior, the Messiah. The Gospels then told the story of His coming and His death for the payment for the sins of the lost. And the book of Acts now describes His empowering of His people to take this message of salvation to a lost world.

You, like the apostles and early believers, have been given the truth—the good news about the only way to God, the message of eternal life, through Jesus Christ. And like these early Christians, you are to share this message with boldness and love. Jesus has promised that His Spirit, the Holy Spirit, will give you the power you need to be His witness. The baton has been handed to you. Take it willingly! And rely on the power and strength of God's indwelling Spirit as you run the race.

From beginning to end,
the Holy Spirit is the operative agent in
the outworking of God's will,
the communication of God's Word, and
the accomplishment of God's purpose. [2]

—*A BIBLE HANDBOOK TO THE ACTS OF THE APOSTLES*

Lesson 2

The Coming of the Holy Spirit

ACTS 2

*H*as anyone made a promise to you they couldn't or didn't keep? Most sincere promises are offered with the greatest of intentions that the promise will be fulfilled. But things happen, many times at no fault of their own, and the one making the promise is not able to fulfill their word.

In Acts chapter 2, we see God the Son, Jesus the risen Savior, fulfill His promise to send the Helper, the Comforter—the Holy Spirit—who will take up permanent residence in those who put their faith in Jesus.

Acts 2 is a progression of God's marvelous promise that the Spirit will be poured out on 120 believers in the upper room. This supernatural power will next be passed on to 3000 people on that same day! This coming of the Holy Spirit will be the catalyst for believers to take the message of the "good news" to the ends of the earth as mandated in Acts 1:8.

God's Message...

There is little doubt among Bible scholars that Luke wrote the Gospel of Luke and the book of Acts. Luke was a highly educated Greek physician (Colossians 4:12-14). His medical training as a keen observer might well explain his use of the word "accurate" (Luke 1:3) in his desire to be precise with his observations.

1. Read Acts 2:1-4 and describe what happened in the room where the disciples gathered.

    The sounds (verses 1-2)—

    The sights (verse 3)—

    The speeches (verse 4)—

2. Read Acts 2:5-13 and describe the crowd's initial responses to the coming of the Holy Spirit as seen in verses 6 and 7.

    One response in verse 6—

    Two responses in verse 7—

    —

—

What were the people amazed about when they heard the fishermen of Galilee speaking (verses 8-10)?

What was the message they were hearing (verse 11)?

How did the people respond?

Verse 12—

Verse 13—

3. Read Acts 2:14-21. How did Peter explain that the disciples were not drunk? (Just a note: The Jewish day started at 6:00 a.m. with the "first hour.")

What was happening, according to the Old Testament prophet Joel (verses 16-21)?

4. Read Acts 2:22-36 and summarize Peter's explanation of what has happened (see verses 32 and 36).

5. Read Acts 2:37-41 and notice the evidence of the crowd's conviction (verse 37). They were:

    —

    —

    What was Peter's twofold command in verse 38?

    —

    —

    What would result from following Peter's instructions (verse 38)?

    —

    —

    After responding to Peter's challenge in verse 40, what happened (verse 41)?

6. Read Acts 2:42-47 and list the four actions of the new believers after they were baptized (verse 42):

    1.

    2.

3.

4.

Read verses 43-47 and enjoy a picture of "body life"—the fellowship of believers. What impresses you the most?

...and Your Heart's Response

- *Emulate the life of the newly formed church.* Look again at the activities of the new believers in Acts 2:44-47. Which aspects of their behavior are you following, and what may be lacking in your church experience?

- *Focus on Christ.* The Jerusalem church was joyous because its singular focus was Jesus Christ. Having just read Acts 2:43-47, how do your behavior and joy match up with those of the early believers? Have you lost some of your excitement for the Savior? Take some time to reflect on your focus and make a note of anything that is diverting your attention away from the Lord. Jot down several changes you plan to make.

- *Do your part.* You cannot miss the fact that every believer seems to have been actively involved in the early church. As a result, the church grew in both quantity and quality. What can you contribute to help make your church a spiritually healthy place that will draw others to Christ? Note one thing you can do or need to do to contribute to your church's body life.

Relying on the Power of the Spirit

Can you imagine? Three thousand people walking and witnessing in unity, empowered by the Holy Spirit? The unity of the believers caused a great stir in Jerusalem. Envision the impact this kind of unity in your own church could have on your community—and even the world! Where does this unity start? With the power of the Spirit working within you as you follow the apostle Paul's admonition

When you strip it of everything else,
Pentecost stands for power and life.
That's what came into the Church when the
Holy Spirit came down on the Day of Pentecost.[3]

—DAVID WILKERSON

Lesson 3

The Giving of
a Second Chance

ACTS 3

ow often do you get a second chance? Probably not very often, right? Few employers, workmates, friends, and even some family members will not allow you to start over. As the golfing term suggests, there aren't many who will give you a "mulligan," a do-over, a second shot. It seems you are stuck with your actions for life.

Maybe that's how Peter, Jesus' disciple, felt after he promised to follow Jesus even if it meant death, and then cowered in fear during Jesus' trial and crucifixion. But Jesus gave Peter a second chance and renewed His trust in Peter (John 21:19). The result? In Acts, we see a changed man! Peter, who was graciously given a second chance by our Lord, is on a mission—a mission to preach and proclaim the resurrection of

Christ. In Acts 2 Peter, filled with the Holy Spirit, stood before hundreds, if not thousands, and delivered his first sermon on the Day of Pentecost.

But Peter was in no way finished. In Acts chapter 3, we discover he has become even bolder. His first sermon was in the streets of Jerusalem. This time, though, Peter boldly stood in the temple area and declared his faith in Jesus.

God's Message...

1. Briefly describe what happened in Acts 3:1-11:

   Who?

   Where?

   When?

   What happened?

   Just a note: This is the first miracle performed by members of the new entity, the church.

2. What was the miracle that created the opportunity for Peter's sermon (Acts 3:11-12)?

3. A good sermon introduction must capture attention, raise a need, and draw the listeners to the subject at hand. How

did Peter, in his second sermon (in Acts 3:12-16), explain the miracle of the lame man who was now standing beside him and John?

4. Read Acts 3:12-16. Peter focused on the person of Jesus in this, his second sermon. List as many words as you can find that Peter used to describe Jesus.

5. In Acts 3:17-21, Peter once again called on his audience to take action. What did he ask of them in verse 19?

    To _____ and to _____

    What three results will occur due to these actions?

    Verse 19—

    Verse 19—

    Verse 20—

6. As you read Acts 3:22-26, keep these points in mind:

    In verses 22-23, Peter is quoting *Moses* to the people. What did Moses predict God would do (verse 22)?

In verses 24-26, *Peter* is speaking to the people. His message is that God fulfilled His prediction in Jesus. According to verse 26, why did God raise up Jesus?

—

—

...and Your Heart's Response

It's so easy to be consumed by the details of events and lose sight of what God wants us to learn and the changes He wants us to make. As you respond to this lesson, think and reflect on these key points from Peter's sermon in Acts chapter 3.

- *Be thankful.* The lame man who was healed praised God and was thankful. Is being thankful a part of your daily life—being thankful to God and to those who help and assist you? Are there any people you want to thank right away?

- *Listen to God's Word.* Peter recites Moses' admonition for the people to "listen to everything he [the Messiah] tells you" (Acts 3:22 NIV). The word "listen" means more than just receiving sounds and words into your ears. The term contains the idea of *hearing with a view toward obeying.* Make it a goal to listen to God's Word when it is read or taught. Then do something about what you hear. This little checklist may help!

___ Take your Bible to church

___ Read along as you hear God's Word

___ Take notes and review them

___ Pray to do what God's message asks of you

Relying on the Power of the Spirit

Today, as you finish reading Peter's sermon and witness the power of the Spirit transforming Peter from a coward to a confident spokesman, think about your life. As with Peter, God has given you a second chance in your second birth. When you received Christ as your Savior, God made you "a new creation; old things have passed away; behold, all things have become new" (2 Corinthians 5:17). Indeed, He has given you a whole new life!

Where does life find you today? Are you a wife? A mom? A sister? A daughter? A daughter-in-law? An awesome auntie? A grandmother? Like Peter, stand with confidence in the roles God has given you. Own your roles and rely on the power of the Spirit to live for and glorify Christ.

The gift of the Spirit is the Spirit Himself,
who regenerates, indwells, unites, and
transforms lives.[4]

—J.A. Alexander

Lesson 4

Demonstrating Power

*L*et the persecution begin! In the first three chapters of Acts, the Jewish leaders had not interfered with the apostles and the fledgling church. Peter and the members of the church had moved freely throughout Jerusalem preaching Jesus as Messiah to anyone who would listen.

The events in Acts 3 began no differently than the days gone by. Peter and John went as usual to the temple to pray and preach. As they were about to enter the temple grounds, the presence of a lame beggar presented an opportunity to demonstrate the power of Jesus as the man, lame from birth, was miraculously made well.

This healed man then followed Peter and John into the temple area, becoming visible proof of the power of the resurrected Jesus. As Peter explained to the assembled crowd, "the faith which comes through Him [Jesus] has given him [the lame man] this perfect soundness in the presence of you all" (Acts 4:16).

It was all good. A great miracle had occurred! The people were listening and believing. The gospel message was displaying its power in the people. But this growing influence began to flame the fires of fierce opposition. In Acts 4 you will see the same authorities who tried, sentenced, and killed a "dangerous" rabbi from Nazareth named Jesus begin seeking to intimidate and silence Jesus' followers.

God's Message...

1. What was Peter's "bottom line" instruction to the people in verse 19?

2. List the groups of Jewish leaders who responded negatively to Peter and John's preaching (Acts 4:1).

   —

   —

   —

3. What was their reaction to Peter's preaching (verse 2)?

   Why were they so upset (verse 2)?

What action did these leaders take (verse 3)?

Just a note: The Sadducees were wealthy, upper-class religious leaders who denied the resurrection of the dead.

4. What was the positive response of many who heard Peter's teaching (verse 4), and how many responded?

5. Read Acts 4:5-12. Who was listed as present for this session...

   ...in verse 5?

   ...in verse 6?

   What did the leaders want to know about the healing of the lame man (verse 7)?

   Before Peter began to answer, what happened (verse 8)?

   Give a short summary of Peter's response (verses 9-11).

   What was Peter's concluding statement in verse 12?

6. Read Acts 4:13-18 for the responses to Peter's message. What did the council determine regarding:

Peter and John (verse 13)?

The lame man's healing (verse 14)?

How to deal with Peter and John (verses 17-18)?

7. Read Acts 4:18-20. How did the apostles respond to the leaders' threats?

8. What happened next in verses 21-22 regarding...
    —the decision of the council, and why?

    —the response of the people?

9. What happened in verses 23-30 regarding the response to Peter and John's report?

10. What happened in verse 31?

11. Read Acts 4:32-35. In a very few words, summarize the further responses of the believers.

Verse 32—

Verse 33—

Verses 34-35—

12. Meet Barnabas. You'll see him again later, but what do you learn about him in verses 36-37?

...and Your Heart's Response

Being filled with the Spirit[5] and controlled by the Spirit requires a daily commitment to obey the commands of Scripture. In Acts 4, those who were filled with the Spirit spoke and witnessed boldly, sacrificed for others, and lived in unity with other believers. Do any of these areas need your attention or need improvement?

- *Pray for the right things.* Persecution was just beginning for the new church. But amazingly, the believers didn't pray for deliverance or safety or peace or a problem-free life. Instead, what did they pray for in verse 29?

What does these believers' focus on "the right things" teach you about your prayers for your day-by-day life and trials?

Relying on the Power of the Spirit

In Acts 4, the result of the believers being filled with the Spirit was thrilling! However, the power of Jesus' Spirit is not always revealed in great miracles and public displays of emotion, but it is definitely displayed in the very act of living. This power is seen in the boldness of your testimony and in your willingness to share with others what God has given you. When you rely on the power of the Spirit, your fears are replaced with boldness, and a coveting heart becomes a giving heart. Now that, my friend, is real power!

The Holy Spirit doesn't need to equip you for what you're not going to do, so if you're in rebellion against Jesus and refusing His right to be Lord, He doesn't need to send the Holy Spirit to equip you for service. And, tragically, you miss out on the joy that He brings. So let the Holy Spirit deal with anything that's keeping you from obeying Christ.[6]

—HENRY T. BLACKABY

Lesson 5

Facing Internal Problems

ACTS 5

Jesus proclaimed, "I will build My church" (Matthew 16:18). In Acts it is evident that Jesus is truly building His church as large numbers of people began professing faith in Him as their long-awaited Messiah.

In this lesson the church is faced with a new kind of problem—dishonesty as people begin to see the church as a place to gain power and be noticed for their "righteous" acts.

How the church leaders handled these emerging problems is crucial because the purity of the church was at stake.

God's Message...

1. Look again at Acts 4:32-37 and summarize in a few words what was happening among the people.

2. Now read Acts 5:1-11. What did Ananias and Sapphira do in verses 1-2?

To whom did Peter attribute this couple's actions?

Peter exposed Ananias and Sapphira's lies and deception. To whom were they lying, according to...

   verse 3?

   verse 4?

These two verses clearly present the Holy Spirit as a person equal with God. How do the verses below reveal the Spirit's deity as equal with God?

   Matthew 28:19—

   1 Corinthians 6:11—

   2 Corinthians 13:14—

What happened in verse 3 of Acts 5?

And in verse 10?

3. Read Acts 5:12-16. After the sudden deaths of Ananias and Sapphira, the apostles continued to preach boldly about Jesus. Briefly describe what was happening in…

   verse 14—

   verses 15-16—

4. Once again the apostles were arrested. They had been warned not to preach about Jesus (Acts 4:18), but with great boldness they continued to witness for Christ. Take a few minutes and read Acts 5:17-45.

   What was the reaction of the Jewish leaders to the apostles' continued preaching (verses 17-18)?

   Briefly describe the miracle that occurred in verses 19-26.

   What was the apostles' response in verse 29 when they were again threatened?

What was the Jewish leadership's initial intent regarding the apostles (verse 33)?

After further discussion, what did the Jewish leaders decide to do instead (verse 40)?

How did the apostles handle their punishment in...

   verse 41?

   verse 42?

...and Your Heart's Response

- *Be ready to obey.* Read Acts 5:19-21. The NIV translation uses the word "immediately" to express the apostles' obedience to the angel's command. When you read God's Word, look carefully for its commands—and obey them. God will give you the grace needed to do what He says, and He will be honored. Can you think of any commands in the Bible you are resisting for fear of pain or conflict?

- *Choose God over others.* Life is full of choices, and you will have to choose whether you obey God or please yourself, your family, your friends, or even those at work. Look again at Acts 5:29 and write out the apostles' words. How can this principle help you choose God's way the next time you have a tempting or compromising choice?

Relying on the Power of the Spirit

It's sobering to realize how easily the enemy Satan (Acts 5:3) can invade your life and compromise your actions! To keep this from happening, be sure you rely on the power of the Spirit. Let the Spirit control you and therefore keep you from evil actions. As Paul pointed out, "Walk in the Spirit" (Galatians 5:16).

It has been almost 2000 years since the events of Acts chapter 5. Jesus is still building His church, and you, as a member of that church, have that same Spirit available to you as you rely on His power.

Acts testifies that the Holy Spirit is a person distinct from but equal to the Father and the Son. He is a person, and He is God.[7]

—*A Bible Handbook to the Acts of the Apostles*

Lesson 6

Choosing a Few Good Men

ACTS 6

hat's alive will grow." This is a truth that covers all of life—from plants, to animals, to humans, and includes the church of Jesus Christ.

In Acts 6 you will see another growth challenge for the church. It was an internal problem that centered on some inconsistencies in the distribution of goods to the needy widows in the congregation. Will this logistical problem cause further dissension? Or will the Spirit-filled apostles solve the problem and the church continue to grow even stronger, or will they be stifled and the church begin to wither?

God's Message...

1. A problem is defined (Acts 6:1)—According to Acts 6:1, what problem surfaced in the newly formed church?

2. A problem is addressed (verses 2-7)—What first step did the apostles take, and what was their concern about themselves (verses 2 and 4)?

    What solution did the church decide upon (verse 3)?

    List the requirements for those who would assist the apostles in solving this problem with the widows (verse 3).

    —

    —

    —

    What action did the apostles take that showed the importance of the seven chosen men and their duties and qualifications (verse 6)?

What were the results of this new approach to ministry in the rapidly growing church (verse 7)?

3. A gifted person is identified (Acts 6:8–7:1)—Look now at Stephen, one of the gifted men whose initial assignment was to "serve tables" and make sure widows received food. Write out what is said about Stephen in...

verse 3—

verse 8—

verse 10—

According to verses 8-10, how did some outside the church respond (that is, what was the result of his ministry)?

Since the opposition could not refute Stephen, what did they do instead? Jot down the tactics of the opposition as seen in...

verse 11—

verse 12—

verse 13—

verse 14—

How is Stephen described in verse 15?

What was the high priest's question to Stephen concerning the accusations against him (Acts 7:1)?

...and Your Heart's Response

- *Do something about your problems.* This chapter addressed a problem that surfaced in the newly emerging church. Problems can arise on every front—at home, in your family, at work, and in the church. What do you learn about managing your problems from the example the apostles set? Review the process they took and formulate a plan for solving your problems.

- *Learn from Stephen's humility and faithfulness.* Stephen's powerful ministry began when he was selected to serve tables and wait on widows because he was a man "of good reputation, full of the Holy Spirit and wisdom" (verse 3).

  Where is God asking you to serve today? Do you fix meals for seven three times a day? Are you a "deaconess" at your church who is called on to help when meals or services are needed? What are you assigned to do for your boss at work? Being filled with the power of the Spirit turns your service—no matter where or to whom—into a ministry. Share one change you can make right away to rely on the Spirit and do your work unto the Lord.

• *Remain calm in unpleasant situations.* Stephen stood before the Jewish council with the Spirit's peace. How do you usually respond to ill treatment and unpleasant situations, and what steps do you need to take to rely on the power—and peace—of the Spirit?

Relying on the Power of the Spirit

The church is to rely on the power of the Spirit, and so is each individual Christian—including you. In Acts 6, we learn God uses people who are walking by the Spirit and relying on His power in every circumstance. You can affect others in your church for good when you are walking by the Spirit. And you can speak with power and wisdom. When you walk by the Spirit you will be a part of the solution—not a part of the problem!

～

*God loves to pour out His Spirit with power
on those who will dare to align radically
their purposes with His.*[8]

—STEVE CHILDERS

Lesson 7

Obeying God Instead of Man

ACTS 7

O n a recent trip to visit my brother and his wife in San Antonio, Texas, Jim and I were treated by them to a visit to the legendary Alamo. Back in 1836, as tensions escalated between Mexico and Texas, Colonel William Travis reportedly pulled out his sword and drew a line in the sand. He then asked for volunteers to cross over the line and join him, understanding that their decision would be irreversible. The legend states that all but one of the defenders joined Travis on his side of the line—and they all died in battle.

The result of their last stand at the Alamo gave the Texas army time to gather troops that ultimately defeated the Mexican army.

Nearly 2000 years before the Alamo, the apostle Peter placed his own "line in the sand" when he challenged his fellow believers who were facing opposition from the Jewish leaders of that day: "We ought to obey God rather than men" (Acts 5:29).

In time, Stephen, who was filled with the Holy Spirit (Acts 6:3), took up Peter's challenge and also stepped across a line.

God's Message...

Acts chapter 7 records Stephen's speech before Israel's religious leaders, which is the first major address of a non-apostle in the book of Acts—as well as the longest one in Acts delivered by anyone—even Peter! Sadly, it is also the first recorded death of a follower and spokesman of Jesus in Acts.

Stephen's speech (Acts 7:2-47) can be divided into three parts:

Part #1: Israel's history as part of God's plans in the world (verses 2-47). Israel's history revolves around three Old Testament saints.

Abraham: Read verses 2-8. What is the most significant feature about the life of Abraham, according to these verses? (Hint: Look at the apostle Paul's citation of Genesis 15:16 in Romans 4:3 for help with this answer.)

Joseph: Read verses 9-19. Describe how God used Joseph's troubles to position him for God's purposes (verse 10).

God had promised Abraham that his descendants would live in Egypt for 400 years. What was the final act that would force the 12 tribes to seek God's help while in Egypt (verses 17-19)?

Moses: Read verses 20-33 and list some of the events in Moses' life that you consider significant for his future role as leader of God's people.

Read verses 33-43 and list some of the issues Moses faced with the rebellious people of Israel.

Part #2: The tabernacle and Solomon's temple as places of worship. Read verses 44-50. Stephen was accused of speaking against the temple and the law. List some of the details that Stephen offered concerning the tabernacle and Solomon's temple and the worship of God.

Part #3: The continued rejection of God's plan by Israel's leadership. Read verses 51-53. What were some of Stephen's accusations?

The reaction of the leaders. Read Acts 7:54,57-58 and list some of the reactions of the leaders.

Stephen's response to their violent behavior. Read verses 55-56 and 59-60 and describe Stephen's appearance and his final remarks toward his murderers.

...and Your Heart's Response

- *Be prepared to speak for Christ.* Stephen was prepared when the opportunity to speak for Christ occurred. He was prepared spiritually—he was filled with the Holy Spirit, and he was prepared with a knowledge of God's dealings with His people.

  How can you be actively preparing yourself spiritually and intellectually to talk to others about your faith in Christ? What can you do today?

  ___Today I will...

  ___One of my goals is...

- *Be assured.* To Moses, God said, "I have surely seen the oppression of My people...[and] have heard their groaning and have come down to deliver them" (Acts 7:34). How does knowing that God sees everything, knows everything, and will act in His own time give you assurance?

Relying on the Power of the Spirit

In our way of thinking, Stephen came to a premature and tragic death. *What a waste, and so young,* you might be thinking. *If he had been able to live longer, just think what he could have done for Jesus!*

Stephen did not have a long ministry before he was martyred, but it was a powerful one with a fantastic ending. Acts 7:56 records that Stephen saw "the heavens open and the Son of Man standing at the right hand of God!" Can you imagine? Stephen provides you with a model and an example of what it means—and looks like—to live for Christ and to be empowered by His Spirit. Do you want your life to have a lasting impact? If so, "obey God rather than men" (Acts 5:29).

*Will God ever ask you to do something you are
not able to do?
The answer is yes—all the time!...
If we function according to our ability alone,
we get the glory;
if we function according to the power of the Spirit
within us, God gets the glory.*[9]

—Henry T. Blackaby

Scattering Through Persecution

ACTS 8

on't you just love living a quiet comfortable life, even if it's only for a day—or an hour? There's nothing like a few moments that are hassle-free. Sounds great, doesn't it? There is just one problem. Jesus had told the disciples to "go therefore and make disciples of all nations" (Matthew 28:19-20). Jesus also said, just before His return to heaven, "You will be my witnesses in Jerusalem and in all Judea and Samaria, and to the end of the earth" (Acts 1:8). This applies to us as well.

The church had fulfilled the first part of Jesus' command to be His "witnesses in Jerusalem," but had stopped with that. But things were about to change. Persecution was about to scatter the church. God was going to force the church to fulfill its mandate to take the gospel to the world. It's been said that "the blood of the martyrs is the seed bed for the expansion of the church." With the death of Stephen, this chapter marks the beginning of that expansion through persecution.

God's Message...

1. Read Acts 8:1-3 and describe how the persecution began. In a few words, what was the context for this persecution, according to Acts 7:54-60?

    After looking at Jesus' instructions in Acts 1:8, describe the initial results of the persecution that began in Acts 8:1.

    What group remained in Jerusalem (verse 1)?

    Who was the chief instrument of this persecution (verses 1 and 3)?

    What was Saul's role in the persecution (verse 3)?

2. Acts 7 described the ministry of Stephen, one of "the seven" men chosen to serve food to widows. Now read Acts 8:4-25 and look at the early stages of the ministry of

Philip, another of "the seven." What was Philip's message to the people of Samaria (verse 5)?

List the miracles that were performed by Philip (verses 6-8).

Who is mentioned in verse 9 as also having an impact on the people, and how is he described?

To whom were his activities attributed and for how long (verses 10-11)?

Describe what happened as a result of Philip's ministry (verses 12-13).

Read verses 14-17 and summarize what took place next.

What was Simon's response when he witnessed others receiving the Holy Spirit at the hands of Peter and John in verses 18-19?

List Peter's fivefold rebuke of Simon in verses 20-23.

Verse 20—

Verse 20—

Verse 21—

Verse 22—

Verse 23—

How did Simon respond to Peter's rebukes (verse 24)?

3. Read 8:26-40 to follow the expansion of the gospel in this next step in God's plan to take the good news to the "end of the earth" (Acts 1:8). God was actively involved in the expansion of His church. Note how God sovereignly directed Philip.

Verses 26-28—

Verse 29—

Verses 39-40—

....and Your Heart's Response

- *Live boldly.* How would you describe your Christian life? Is it dull and routine? Are you experiencing any persecution? If your Christian life is unchallenged, it may mean you are not very vocal or bold about your faith. Read again Acts 1:8 and write down one thing you can do to reach your "Jerusalem" this week.

- *How open are you to God's leading?* Throughout chapter 8 Philip was continually led by God to specific acts of witnessing and evangelism—first to the Samaritans, and then to the Ethiopian man. Each time, Philip boldly took advantage of the opportunity to share his faith. How open are you to sharing your faith through normal daily life situations? Write out a short prayer asking God to open your eyes and heart to opportunities to share your faith with those who are lost.

Relying on the Power of the Spirit

Simon wanted Peter's power and the gifts and abilities Peter and John exhibited. Do you ever wish for an ability that would put you in the limelight or give you more prestige? You will never exhibit spiritual power if you are trying to manifest spiritual gifts you don't possess. Remember this: God doesn't make mistakes. You have the exact, specific gifts and talents you need to serve Him! Thank God for what He has given *you*, and rely on His Spirit to empower what you have for His purposes.

We are to come to the Word in a spirit of humility and contrition because we recognize that we are sinful, that we are often blind to our sinfulness, and that we need the enlightening power of the Holy Spirit in our hearts.[10]

—JERRY BRIDGES

Witnessing God's Grace

ACTS 9

The word *grace* can be defined as God's unmerited favor. We as sinners deserve death (Romans 6:23) but God, in His great mercy, has offered His grace to those He saves. What a blessed reality!

In Acts 9, you will witness God's grace in the life of a man named and referred to as "Saul of Tarsus," later to become the apostle Paul, and you will witness God's grace as one man is healed, and a beloved saint is raised from the dead. God's grace is truly sufficient (2 Corinthians 12:9)!

God's Message...

In Acts, chapters 1–7 describe the preaching of the gospel in Jerusalem. Chapter 8 shows us believers who are under the threat of persecution taking the good news of Jesus to

Judea and Samaria. Now in chapter 9 we see the transition to the spread of the gospel "to the end of the earth" through Saul, an amazing servant of God.

1. Read Acts 9:1-19 for the account of Saul's conversion. What was Saul doing when we last read about him in Acts 8:1 and 3?

   Describe Saul's present mission in Acts 9:1-2.

   List some key events that occurred on the road to Damascus.

      Verse 3–

      Verses 4-5—

      Verse 6—

      Verse 7—

   Once Saul arrived in Damascus, what happened (verses 8-9)?

   Describe the man named Ananias and his involvement in Saul's life in…

verse 10—

verses 11-12—

verses 13-14—

verses 15-16—

What was Ananias's twofold purpose in verse 17?

—

—

Note the results reported in...

verse 18—

verse 19—

2. Read Acts 9:20-31. What was Saul's new message, and where did he proclaim it (verse 20)?

What did the people wonder regarding Saul's actions, and what did Saul do (verses 21-22)?

Briefly summarize the information recorded in...

verse 23—

verse 24—

verse 25—

According to Galatians 1:17-18, what happened to Saul after leaving Damascus?

There was a period of at least three years between Saul's conversion and his trip to Jerusalem. What was the response to Saul's arrival in Jerusalem in Acts 9:26?

Who finally acted as Saul's "sponsor" and how did he convince the leaders in Jerusalem of Saul's credibility (verse 27)?

Compare the reaction to Saul's preaching in Jerusalem (verses 28-30) with the reaction in Damascus (verses 22-25).

Verse 31 is a church growth report. Where were the churches located?

List the fivefold description of the healthy churches in verse 31.

—   —

—   —

—

3. Read Acts 9:32-43. What happened in Lydda in verses 33-35?

    Describe what was also happening in Joppa, a town about ten miles from Lydda (verses 36-42), and mention as well the people's response.

...and Your Heart's Response

*   *Don't wait until you think you are ready.* Many believers feel they need to wait until they are thoroughly grounded in their faith before venturing out to share the gospel. What insights about witnessing and evangelism can you learn from reading Acts 9:19-22?

- *Break down barriers*. As a devout Jew, Peter was for-
  bidden from having contact with dead animals. Yet he
  stayed with "Simon, a tanner" (9:43) whose occupation
  involved handling dead animals and animal skins. Peter's
  initial prejudice toward others was beginning to break
  down as God prepared him for meeting with Cornelius,
  a Gentile Roman soldier, in chapter 10. Can you pinpoint
  any biases you may have toward those who are not like
  you or who have different customs and beliefs? Note them,
  pray, and remove them.

Relying on the Power of the Spirit

In Acts 9:31 we see the church enjoying a time of peace
and growth due to the empowering ministry of the Holy
Spirit. Like the early church, when you are filled with the
Spirit, you will display the grace of God and the power of
the risen Jesus. And you will have the peace that the early
church enjoyed. You will be a walking advertisement for the
Savior.

The fruit of the Spirit is…peace (GALATIANS 5:22).

Spreading of the Gospel to the Gentiles

ACTS 10

et ready for change! In the first nine chapters of Acts the ministry of the Spirit was mostly reserved for the Jews and Samaritans. Suddenly chapter 10 of Acts describes the Spirit's activity in a Gentile—yes, a Gentile—army officer and his household, and things are about to change.

With the coming of the Holy Spirit upon the Gentiles, the mystery of the church is completed. The "middle wall of separation" between Jew and Gentile has been broken down (Ephesians 2:14). From this point on, we realize that in the church, the Lord Jesus has "created in Himself one new man from the two, thus making peace" (Ephesians 2:14-15).

God's Message...

As you work your way through chapter 10, you will continue to see Jesus sovereignly directing the expansion of His church. With the conversion of one Roman centurion and his household, a significant step was made: Jesus was fulfilling His promise to send the "good news" to the ends of the earth (Acts 1:8).

1. Read Acts 10:1-8 and answer these questions to discover the events leading up to Cornelius sending for Peter. What was Cornelius's profession and rank (verse 1)?

    Just a note: A centurion commanded 100 soldiers. Some texts describe Cornelius's rank as "captain" (NIV). This position was highly regarded by the Roman army.

    List the fourfold description of Cornelius's character found in verse 2.

    —

    —

    —

    —

    Describe Cornelius's heavenly vision by reading verses 3-8 and answering these questions. Who appeared, and at what time?

Just a note: The normal times for Jewish prayers were at the third hour (6:00 a.m.) and the ninth hour (3:00 p.m.), the times of the morning and evening sacrifices.

What was the angel's commendation...

...and the angel's direction?

What was Cornelius's response?

2. Read Acts 10:9-18. What do you learn about Peter's vision in verses 10-13?

When did Peter have his vision (verse 9)? See also verses 1-8.

Just a note: Praying three times a day was not commanded in Scripture, but Peter followed the example of pious men who lived before him by adding the noonday prayer (see Daniel 6:10).

Why was Peter objecting to the message of the vision when God commanded him to "kill and eat" (verse 14)?

How did God respond to Peter's hesitation (verse 15)?

How many times was this vision repeated (verse 16)?

3. Read Acts 10:19-33 for details regarding Peter's visit to Cornelius. Who reassured Peter that he should go with the three strangers when they arrived (verses 19-20)?

How did Cornelius's men describe Cornelius, and what occurred that caused him to send his messengers to ask Peter to come to his home (verses 21-22)?

Later, how does Peter further explain why he was willing to meet with the Gentiles (verses 28-29)?

How does this assurance demonstrate the ministry of the Holy Spirit as recorded in John 16:13?

What did Peter experience when he arrived at Cornelius's house (Acts10:23-27)?

4. Read Acts 10:34-43, Peter's sermon to the Gentile audience who gathered in Cornelius's home. In verse 43, how did Peter sum up the reason Jesus came to Earth?

5. Note the different responses to Peter's sermon in verses 44-48.

    —The Holy Spirit's response (verse 44)

    —The response of the Jewish believers ("the circumcision") who came with Peter from Joppa (verse 45)

    —The Gentiles' response (verse 45)

    —Peter's response (verses 46-48)

Just a note: Theologian John Phillips writes this explanation of speaking "with tongues":

> This sign gift was necessary. Peter and the other Jews would probably have never received the Gentiles as "fellow heirs" (Ephesians 3:6) apart from this sign. That, of course, is in keeping with the basic purpose of the gift of tongues, which was to bear witness against the unbelief of the Jewish people as seen on its first occasion in Acts 2.[11]

...and Your Heart's Response

- *Look for seekers.* Sometimes people will seek you out to hear the truth about Jesus. That's what Cornelius did—he reached out to Peter. Like Peter, be prepared to share the gospel when others turn to you. But it's also important that you look for seekers. Jesus came to seek and to save the lost. Look at Luke 19:1-10 and make notes on how Jesus treated a seeker named Zacchaeus.

- *Beware of prejudice!* Peter, like every devout Jew, was raised to shun all contact with Gentiles. His prejudice was strong, and it took a vision from heaven and the voice of God to help him break down a serious barrier—a barrier that would keep him from sharing God's love for all humanity with non-Jews.

  What feelings of prejudice toward people who maybe don't look like you, think like you, act like you, or believe like you are you carrying around? Or what signs of prejudice have you observed in other Christians?

  Remember, *"God so loved the world* that He gave His only begotten Son, that whoever believes in Him should not perish but have everlasting life"* (John 3:16). Don't let the barriers of prejudice or a lack of love and forbearance for all mankind keep you from sharing with others about the love God has for you, a sinner.

Relying on the Power of the Spirit

Peter's words to Cornelius and his family were sincere, heartfelt, and accurate. However, they would have been powerless without the Holy Spirit working in the hearts of Peter's listeners. This is a good reminder as you share your faith. Results do not depend on how well you can articulate the gospel message or your vast wealth of biblical knowledge. Rather, they depend on the Spirit, who does the real convincing and convicting.

∽

If a person is filled with the Holy Spirit,
his witness will not be optional or mandatory—
it will be inevitable.[12]

—RICHARD HALVERSON

Lesson 11

Experiencing the Spirit's Work

ACTS 11

The book of Acts is a book of transition and change. Change is hard for most people to handle. We tend to like the way things have always been. It's comfortable and predictable. But the Christian life cannot remain static. Christians are either growing, changing, and being conformed to the image of Christ or they are sliding back into old habits.

The Jews of the early church were having a hard time adjusting to the changes God's Spirit was producing in them. It took some time for Peter and others to realize and respond to what God was doing. And still there was resistance and misunderstanding, as you will see in Acts 15. But for now, let's experience the Spirit's work as the gospel message moves out from Judea like a mighty wave toward the Gentile world.

God's Message...

1. Read Acts 11:1-18. As you read, remember God asked Peter to share Christ with Gentiles—who believed and received the Holy Spirit!

   Read Acts 11:1-3 and note why the Jewish believers in Jerusalem were upset with Peter.

   Read Acts 11:4-15 and note Peter's account of his actions.

   How did Peter justify his actions (verses 16-17)?

   After all that Peter said, what was the response of his critics (verse 18)?

2. Read Acts 11:19-26 to learn about Barnabas and the growth of the new believers at Antioch. Keep in mind that to show that Peter's encounter with Cornelius was not an exception, Acts 11 shines the spotlight on the widespread movement of the Spirit of God that ultimately focused on the important city of Antioch. What event launched the movement of the gospel away from Jerusalem (verse 19)?

   List the places mentioned as the gospel message was carried beyond Jerusalem. If possible, look at these places on a Bible atlas.

—

—

—

What initial audience was targeted as the gospel was shared (verse 19)?

As the disciples moved away from their strong Jewish heritage, their adherence to Old Testament law, and the use of the Hebrew language, what happened, and what were the results (verses 20-21)?

With the Hellenists' interest and response, the church leaders in Jerusalem sent Barnabas to investigate. (Hellenists were generally non-Greeks who had adopted the Greek language and culture as their own.) What did Barnabas immediately do when he saw for himself what God was doing among the Gentiles (verse 23)?

How is Barnabas described in verse 24?

After witnessing firsthand the grace of God and the many believers in Antioch, what did Barnabas do about the growth and the needs of the church in Antioch (verse 25)?

How long did Saul and Barnabas minister together, and what was the focus of their ministry (verse 26)?

3. Read Acts 11:27-30 to see generosity as a demonstration of spiritual maturity. What was the impending crisis as presented by the prophet Agabus in verses 27-28?

How did the individual believers respond to the news (verse 29)?

How was their gift sent to those in need (verse 30)?

Fast forward: What is the prophet Agabus doing the next time he appears in Acts (Acts 21:10-11)?

...and Your Heart's Response

- *Build a common bridge.* The men of Cyprus and Cyrene, who spoke Greek, went to Antioch and "spoke to the Hellenists" in their own language, Greek, thus building a bridge for sharing the gospel. How could the practice of building a common bridge—a key principle of evangelism—improve your outreach strategy?

- *Involve others in your ministry.* Barnabas shows us that ministry involves teamwork. Every believer has spiritual gifts and unique strengths and abilities. Rather than single-handedly taking on the ministry to the new believers in Antioch, Barnabas set out to find Paul to help him. What can you learn about humility from the ministry of Barnabas in Antioch, and about your outlook on your ministry?

- *Give from your abundance.* The believers in Antioch gave "according to their ability." There was a crisis and there was a need. And they acted! How does your heart attitude toward giving to those in need compare to that of these believers in Acts 11? What can you do to change your giving patterns—and your attitude toward the needs of others?

Relying on the Power of the Spirit

Barnabas was described as "a good man, full of the Holy Spirit and of faith." What was the result of his Spirit-empowered life? The Bible says, "A great many people were added to the Lord" (verse 24)! And Barnabas was willing to share the spotlight and seek the assistance of others. Do you want your life to have this kind of power and impact—the Spirit's kind of power and impact? Then follow Barnabas's example:

Take care of the depth of your spiritual life.
Walk by the Spirit.
Seek all the help you can get.
Trust God for the results.

When you tend to these four spiritual responsibilities that nurture the *depth* of your relationship with God, God will take care of the *breadth* of your ministry.

A person filled with the Holy Spirit will be
a person Christlike in character, conduct and
conversation.[13]

—JOHN PHILLIPS

Lesson 12

Continuing the Refining Process

ACTS 12

ave you ever seen a speeding car with the bumper sticker that says, "Please be patient—God isn't finished with me yet!"? Seeing that driver breaking the law probably had you thinking, *God sure has a long way to go with that person!*

If that lawbreaking driver is a child of God, then the theology of the bumper sticker is correct. From the moment of your salvation, God is in the process of conforming you into the image of your Savior Jesus Christ. Even though there are momentary lapses in your conduct, the transforming work of the Holy Spirit will continue until you see Jesus face-to-face. How does this process take place in your life? God uses people, events, and circumstances to refine you.

In Acts chapter 12, you will continue to see the refining work of the Holy Spirit in the lives of the Jewish believers in and around Jerusalem. The emphasis in Acts will soon shift to the apostle Paul and the Gentile church, but God is not finished with the church in Jerusalem.

God's Message...

1. Read Acts 12:1-4, which reveals yet more persecution of believers in Christ. Who are the people named in these verses?

   Briefly state what was happening.

   Where and when was it happening?

   Bonus question. There are four generations of Herods named in the New Testament. What actions were attributed to each Herod named below?

   Herod the Great (Matthew 2:16)—

   Herod the tetrarch (Matthew 14:1-12)—

   Herod the king (Acts 12:1-4)—

Herod Agrippa (Acts 25:13-22)—

2. Read Acts 12:5-19 and describe the actions and reactions of the people involved in this passage.

The church in Jerusalem (verse 5)—

Peter (verse 6)—

Peter in the presence of the angel (verses 7-10)—

Peter's realization (verse 11)—

Peter's next move (verse 12)—

The church members (verses 12-16)—

Peter's instructions (verse 17)—

Herod's actions (verses 18-19)—

3. Read Acts 12:20-25 to see how God dealt with Herod and continued His plans for the expansion of the church. In your own words, briefly share what happened in these verses.

What effect did the death of James, the imprisonment of Peter, the persecution of believers, and the death of Herod have on the church (Acts 12:24)?

In spite of much adversity, how do you see more growth taking place in the church in verse 25?

...and Your Heart's Response

- *Accept the fact of God's sovereignty.* James and Peter were both apostles and both a part of Jesus' inner circle. Yet one died and the other lived. Furthermore, the same occurred in the lives of Stephen and Philip: Stephen was stoned to death early in his ministry, and Philip had a long life and a far-reaching productive ministry.

  There are no human explanations for the differences. The only explanation is the sovereignty of God, the divine purpose God has for each of His children. How does Acts 13:36 help explain God's actions: "For David, after he had served the purpose of God in his own generation, fell asleep"?

- *Influence your family.* The Herods left behind a legacy of evil. They are among the most extreme examples of evil, but it is good to constantly ask yourself, "What kind of example am I setting for my children?" Ask it now. Then determine what changes you can and must make in your parenting. List one immediate change here.

- *Pray in faith.* Read again the church's reaction to Peter's escape in verses 13-16. How serious are you in your belief that prayer is necessary, vital, and a responsibility? Do you really believe that God hears your prayers? That prayer makes a difference? That prayer changes things? How should such beliefs affect your prayer life?

Relying on the Power of the Spirit

Paul and Barnabas had been sent on a mission to Jerusalem, and Scripture says the two of them "fulfilled their ministry" (verse 25). How did this occur? They relied on the power of the Spirit and they prayed constantly.

People, events, and circumstances affect you in one of two ways: Either they become stepping stones to progress or they become barriers—their effect is all in your response. One response propels you, while the other diverts you. What mission has God given you? Are you a wife? A mom? A daughter? A missionary? A teacher? Are you holding down a job? First pray! Then name your mission, and own it. Ask for the Spirit's help in not being distracted or diverted from the mission God has given you.

The Holy Spirit always has His way in the end. He does not force His will, He does not coerce; He remains invisible, inaudible, but infinite, inescapable, and infallible, guiding all things to work out His sovereign will.[14]

—JOHN PHILLIPS

Lesson 13

Recognizing God's Call

ACTS 13

As you step into this lesson, keep in mind Acts 13 occurs only a few years after Herod's persecution of the believers, which caused believers to leave Jerusalem. Many settled in Antioch. In time the church there grew and had a great lineup of outstanding teachers, including Barnabas and Paul.

Now let's see what God, the Holy Spirit, asks of the believers in Antioch to cause them to continue Jesus' mandate to spread the gospel (Acts 1:8). How responsive will they be? Read on to discover the answers.

God's Message...

1. Read Acts 13:1-3. What activities were the leaders of the church in Antioch participating in when the Spirit spoke (verse 2)?

   What did the Spirit instruct them to do (verse 2)?

   How did the group respond in verse 3?

   Just a note: See Acts 6:6 for a similar ceremony. In both situations the "laying on of hands" signified affirmation, support, and identification with their proposed ministries, not the bestowal of additional spiritual power.

2. Read Acts 13:4-12. What was the clue that the mission would be successful (verse 4)?

   Looking at verses 4-5, who joined Paul and Barnabas to complete this missionary team (see also 12:25)?

   As this group launched their ministry, where did they begin proclaiming the word of God (verse 5)?

   Describe Paul's spiritual condition as he confronted a false prophet (verse 9).

From verse 11 recount what Paul said would happen—and what did happen—to Elymas the magician.

Carefully read verse 12 and then state what moved the proconsul to believe.

3. Read Acts 13:13-15. What change occurred in the missionary team (verse 13)?

Once again, what was the preaching strategy as the team moved on to the island of Cyprus (verses 14-15)?

Just a note: Often a guest to the synagogue was asked to teach. Very few, if any, were better qualified to teach than Paul, the former Pharisee who had been tutored by Gamaliel, a great rabbi in Jerusalem (Acts 22:3).

4. Read Acts 13:16-41. This is Paul's first recorded sermon, which opens with a brief historical summary of God's dealings with the Jewish nation (verses 16-22). What shift in emphasis do you notice in verses 21-23?

What event is the major focus of the final part of Paul's sermon beginning in verse 30?

5. Read Acts 13:42-52. What was the response of the people after Paul's sermon (verse 42)?

What happened on the following Sabbath (verse 44)?

How did the Jews respond to Paul's second sermon (verse 45)?

What was Paul's response to the Jewish opposition, according to verses 46-47?

How does verse 48 speak to the fact of God's sovereignty in salvation?

According to Ephesians 2:8 what part do you play in your salvation?

...and Your Heart's Response

- *Listen when God's Word is taught.* Paul reminded his audience that the people in Jerusalem heard the prophets read every Sabbath. Yet they failed to heed their message.

  How focused are you when hearing the truth preached every week at church? Look up Matthew 13:43b and write it here.

- *Revisit the resurrection.* The resurrection was of utmost importance to the early church, and the focal point of Paul's preaching. Briefly state why the resurrection of Jesus is so important for building your faith, according to 1 Corinthians 15:14-19.

- *Beware of envy.* According to Acts 13:44-45, envy was the reason for the attacks on the mission team. When you see others succeeding where you have not, or when others receive the affirmation you crave, do you become envious? What response should you have to the success of others?

Relying on the Power of the Spirit

Acts 13 gives a beginning history of the choosing, sending, and ministry of the first official missionary team. What was this missionary team's secret? First, they were sensitive to the Spirit's instructions to leave the security of the church. Second, they were filled with the Spirit and spoke and acted boldly. Third, they continued in the power of the Holy Spirit (verse 52). The common theme through all this was a continuous reliance on the Spirit. As you recognize and answer God's call and rely on the Spirit's leading, you will fulfill God's will.

> *Being filled with the Spirit is living in the conscious presence of the Lord Jesus Christ, letting His mind, through the Word, dominate everything that is thought and done.*[15]

—JOHN MACARTHUR

Lesson 14

Continuing to Bear Fruit

ACTS 14

*I*n my library I have an entire section reserved for biographies of great men and women of faith who have served our Lord as missionaries and spokespersons. Between the covers of these records of their service are also the details of their trials, sufferings, deprivations, and the persecution many of these saints encountered. As I am working my way through Acts, I can't help but recall so many of these missionaries' experiences as you and I are continuing to read and learn about persecution—the persecution of the church at large, and the persecution of certain individuals.

In our last lesson we saw missionaries Paul and Barnabas enduring persecution in Antioch. Now let's follow along as this duo of full-of-faith missionaries continues their journey into the heart of the region of Galatia. Keep your eyes open for the many ways they are persecuted. And don't fail to notice that God's message spoken from their lips continued to bear fruit!

God's Message...

1. Paul and Barnabas in Antioch (Acts 13:48-52)

    Read again Acts 13:48-51. What was the negative reaction to Paul and Barnabas's time in Antioch of Pisidia?

    These two missionaries left behind two completely different groups, one of which clearly rejected them (verse 50). How is the second group described in verse 48?

    Just a note: The term "disciples" could refer to Paul and Barnabas, or to the new converts at Antioch, or to both. In this lesson you will see the term *disciples* used to refer to the new converts.

2. Paul and Barnabas in Iconium (Acts 14:1-7)

    What were the two responses to their message in the synagogue?

    Verse 1—

    Verse 2—

    What was the response of the missionaries, according to verse 3?

What prompted the missionary team's departure from Iconium (verses 4-7)?

3. Paul and Barnabas in Lystra (Acts 14:7-20)

   Just a note: Lystra (verse 7) was about 18 miles from Iconium and was the home of Lois, Eunice, and Timothy (Acts 16:1-2). No synagogue is mentioned here, so the apostles most likely preached to a crowd gathered in the marketplace.

   Describe the miracle that occurred (verses 8-10).

   Read verses 11-12. What did the people assume?

   According to verse 13, what did the people attempt to do?

   How did the apostles respond (verses 14-18)?

4. Paul and Barnabas on their way home (Acts 14:22-25)

   Derby (verse 20) was the most distant point of Paul and Barnabas's first missionary journey. What was their two-fold mission as they began retracing their steps?

   Verse 22—

Verses 23-25—

5. Paul and Barnabas in Antioch (Acts 14:26-28)

What was the first order of business upon their return home (verse 26-27)?

Just a note: Most Bible scholars believe Paul wrote the epistle of Galatians while in Antioch (verse 28).

...and Your Heart's Response

• *Make your message fit*—Paul was a master at sharing the gospel because he sought to make his message fit with the people's knowledge and perception of God. For an example, see verses 15-17.

You live in a post-Christian era and your next-door neighbor probably has little or no knowledge of the God of the Bible. Can you come up with any ideas about how you could approach your neighbors or workmates? Jot them down and begin praying for an opportunity!

• *Face opposition*—Like Paul and Barnabas, as a Christian, you are called by God to live boldly for Jesus, share the good news, and accept any ridicule and rejection that come your way. Thanks to God's grace, which is always sufficient, you can face persecution with power (2 Corinthians 12:9), confidence, and joy, knowing that you have been "counted worthy to suffer shame for His name" (Acts 5:41). How do Paul and Barnabas encourage you as you face the potential for a negative response in your community?

Relying on the Power of the Spirit

Most Christians don't go on extended mission trips to foreign lands. But wherever you are, you can do as Paul and Barnabas did: They spoke "boldly in the Lord" (verse 3). Don't give up sharing the gospel message! Do your part and sow the message of the good news, and leave the convincing and fruitbearing to the Holy Spirit.

Then, when or if you have to move, the fruit of your ministry remains. While angry mobs drove out the servants of God, they could not drive out the Spirit of God.

> *Abide in Me, and I in you. As the branch cannot bear fruit of itself, unless it abides in the vine, neither can you, unless you abide in Me. I am the vine, you are the branches. He who abides in Me, and I in him, bears much fruit; for without Me you can do nothing* (John 15:4-5).

Discussing Law and Grace

Whew! It's been quite an adventure traveling alongside Paul and Barnabas. What a pair! It's been a privilege to learn from their character, dedication, and how they managed problems and persecution.

Having finished their first missionary tour, these two men returned to their sending church in Antioch, where they resumed their roles as teachers and leaders. During their time in Antioch, men came from Jerusalem teaching that the believers in Antioch, who were mainly Gentiles, were missing a step in salvation. These false teachers taught that Gentiles must first become Jews before they can be saved. They preached that Christ plus Judaism equals salvation.

God's Message...

Right away in Acts 15, Paul and Barnabas were sent to Jerusalem to inquire whether these teachers and their message represented the thinking of the apostles and elders in Jerusalem. The outcome of their trip to meet with the council in Jerusalem will determine the future of the Christian movement. Those attending and assembled at this council meeting would answer the question "How does a person attain salvation? Is it by grace alone, or grace plus the law—grace plus works?"

1. The reason for a trip to Jerusalem (Acts 15:1-4)

   What is the issue presented in verse 1 that led to Paul and Barnabas traveling to Jerusalem?

   How did Paul and Barnabas and the church at Antioch respond to these teachers' message (verses 2)?

   Describe the ministry that occurred on their 300-mile journey from Antioch to Jerusalem (verse 3).

   What report did the Antioch delegation give when they arrived in Jerusalem (verse 4)?

2. The opening remarks of the council (Acts 15:5-18)

   What issue was raised in verse 5, and by whom?

Who would settle the argument between salvation by grace and salvation by works (verse 6)?

Peter's defense—What did Peter point out from his personal experience in order to defend salvation by grace (verses 7-11)?

Paul and Barnabas's defense—What did these two men share from their personal experiences to convince the council that Gentiles are part of Christ's church (verse 12)?

James's defense—What argument for grace did James use to affirm Peter's experience with the Gentiles (verses 13-18)?

3. The resolution of the council (Acts 15:19-21)

Write out the elements of James's conclusion in...

verse 19—

verse 20—

Why did James give these restrictions (verse 21)?

4. The resolve of the council (Acts 15:22-34)

   What was the council's first decision (verse 22)?

   What was the council's second decision (verse 23)?

   What did the letter written by the apostles, elders, and brethren in Jerusalem say about the false teachers who had traveled to Antioch (verses 24-27)?

   What words imply that God was clearly leading in this decision (verses 28-29)?

   In verses 32-35, what ministries did the members of the delegation from Jerusalem have among the believers?

...and Your Heart's Response...

- *Beware of adding to your faith.* Unfortunately there is a bit of legalism, or "Pharisee-ism," in all of us. Legalism is anything that goes beyond what is prescribed in Scripture. It's easy to unwittingly uphold denominational traditions, church-worship structure, and external legal requirements as necessary elements to your faith. Take a spiritual inventory of your attitudes and actions as a Christian. Can you

think of anything that is taking away from your freedom
in Christ?

* *Respond to authority.* The decisions by the Jerusalem
  council had great potential for trouble. Both sides were
  very committed to their beliefs. And yet the people submitted to the instructions of the leaders, thereby pre-
  venting a "church split" and the forming of factions.
  Here's something to think about: God has pledged to hold
  church leaders accountable for their decisions, and He
  holds you accountable for how well you submit to their
  authority.

Relying on the Power of the Spirit

The solution to an extremely serious problem in Acts 15
sounds too good to be true, doesn't it? There was a problem,
the leaders met, drew conclusions, formulated a plan, and
acted on it.

How could this happen? Our answer to this phenomenal
and peaceful resolution is in verse 28: "It seemed good to
the Holy Spirit, and to us [the leaders]..." The Holy Spirit led,
and the leaders responded. The result? The people in the
church in Jerusalem submitted to the decision of the council,
thereby presenting a unified church that modeled Christ's
love and a sense of order and stability to a watching world.

How you respond to the decisions made by the leaders
in your church will demonstrate to the world the real character of your church and of your own spiritual maturity.

*We may rely upon the Holy Spirit
to give us understanding of the Word of God, and
to guide us into his will for us.*[16]

—MILLARD J. ERICKSON

Being Sensitive to the Spirit

ACTS 15:36–16:40

*T*here is no evidence that the apostle Paul was ever married or had children. But Paul possessed all the emotions and concerns for his associates, disciples, and every child of God that parents have for their children. When false teachers began messing with "his children" in Galatia, Paul immediately wrote them a letter—the book of Galatians—as a first step in protecting his children from false teaching.

When Paul was ready to hit the road for a personal visit to Galatia to check on his children in the faith, a "team" problem arose. Barnabas wanted to reinstate his nephew, John Mark, as a team member, but Paul disagreed strongly because John Mark had deserted them in the past. All progress stood still until this problem could be faced—and solved.

God's Message...

1. The parting of two missionaries (Acts 15:36-41)

   Read Acts 15:36-41 to discover the core problem between Paul and Barnabas.

   Verse 37—Barnabas wanted...

   Verse 38—Paul did not want...

   What had John Mark done in the past (verse 38; see also Acts 13:13)?

   In the end, what did Barnabas do (verse 39)?

   What did Paul do (verses 40-41)?

2. Paul's second missionary journey (Acts 16:1-5)

   Describe what qualified young Timothy for consideration for Paul's mission team.

   His lineage (verse 1)—

   His character (verse 2)—

   Why did Paul want Timothy to be circumcised (verse 3)?

3. The call from Macedonia (Acts 16:6-10)

   How did God direct Paul and his team in...

   verse 6?—

   verse 7?—

   verses 8-9?—

   What was Paul's conclusion and immediate response after receiving the vision (verse 10)?

4. The response of Lydia in Philippi (Acts 16:11-15)

   What occurred on the Sabbath day (verse 13)?

   Describe the woman Lydia (verse 14):

   Her profession—

   Her hometown—

   Her spirituality—

   Her twofold response to salvation (verse 15)—

   —

—

5. The people's response to the missionaries (Acts 16:16-40)

When Paul's team encountered a slave girl (verse 16), what did she announce to the people (verse 17)?

What was Paul's response to the girl and her behavior (verse 18)?

What was the response of the girl's owners (verses 19-21)?

What was the response of the town's officials and its citizens (verses 21-23)?

6. The responses of those in the prison (Acts 16:23-26)

What a scene occurred inside the prison in Philippi! How did the following people and groups respond to the events that occurred?

The Philippian jailer (verses 23-24)—

The missionaries (verse 25)—

The other prisoners (verse 25)—

The prison itself (verse 26)—

What was the result of all that occurred within the prison walls (verse 26)?

7. The Philippian jailer's response (Acts 16:27-34)

His first response (verse 27)—

What kept the jailer from following through on his initial assumption (verse 28)?

His question (verses 29-30)—

How did Paul and Silas answer the jailer's question (verses 31-32)?

What was the jailer's response to the truth of the Word of the Lord (verses 33-34)?

8. The response of the authorities (Acts 16:35-40)

The authorities' wishes (verses 35-36)—

Note Paul's demand and the authorities' response (verses 37-39)—

What was the team's final act in Philippi (verse 40)?

...and Your Heart's Response

- *Agree to disagree.* Both Paul and Barnabas had good reasons why John Mark should and should not join them on a new missionary journey. The Bible does not comment on who was right or wrong. Yet even though they disagreed, they did not allow their disagreement to table their ministry and cease their mission work. What lessons do you learn here about resolving conflicts with your brothers and sisters in Christ?

- *Make mentoring a key ministry.* Paul and Barnabas each took a new disciple to mentor and train. In time, both John Mark and Timothy went on to play major roles in the early church. Mentoring is vital to the church. What guidelines do you find in Titus 2:3-5 for mentoring younger women?

Relying on the Power of the Spirit

We are not told how the Holy Spirit told Paul that he and his team should go in a certain direction. But as circumstances arose and as Paul was sensitive to the Spirit's leading, their team eventually arrived at Troas. Paul then received a vision in which the team was given further specific instructions.

What decision are you facing today? The Holy Spirit is willing to give you directions for your life and ministry. He will lead you as you pray, as you search the Scriptures for His guidelines, and as you live as a woman after God's own heart—a woman who desires to do all God's will (Acts 13:22).

...the Spirit is not given only to those who "have it all together" but to the rest of us so that we might be able to "get it all together."[17]

—Erwin and Rebecca Lutzer

Lesson 17

Altering Your Strategy
ACTS 17

Change and adjustments are not a bad thing. In fact, most time management experts will tell you to regularly evaluate your life and make corrections so that you can keep moving forward in whatever you do.

Like most people, the apostle Paul was a creature of habit. He had a system for preaching the gospel. He would first go to the local synagogues and preach to the Jews, and any God-fearing Greeks in attendance. The response to his approach was always the same—a few Jews believed in Jesus as Messiah, there was a great response among the Greeks, and many times a riot occurred! But in Acts 17 we see Paul altering his strategy when he preached to a purely Greek audience.

God's Message...

1. Paul and Silas in Thessalonica (Acts 17:1-9)

    Chapter 17 picks up with Paul and his team leaving Luke in Philippi to assist the newly established church there. The team led by Paul and Silas journeyed about 100 miles until they arrived at the city of Thessalonica.

    According to verse 2, how long was the team in Thessalonica?

    What was Paul's message (verse 3)?

    Describe the response of those in verse 4.

    Describe the response of others in verses 5-9.

    —the Jews (verse 5)

    —the mob (verses 5-6)

    —the accusations made by the mob (verses 6-9)

    —against Jason and the brethren

    —against Paul and the missionaries

2. Paul and Silas in Berea (Acts 17:10-15)

When and how did the brethren in Thessalonica assist Paul and Silas (verse 10)?

Where was Paul's next stop...and where did he immediately go (verse 10)?

What two things set the Bereans apart from those in Thessalonica in their response to the preaching of the Word (verse 11)?

—

—

List the kinds of people who responded positively to Paul's preaching (verse 12).

Describe what happened next (verses 13-14).

Due to pressing circumstances, what did the brethren do to help Paul (verse 14)?

Who remained in Thessalonica, and why (verses 14-15)?

What instructions were given regarding Silas and Timothy (verse 15)?

3. Paul in Athens (Acts 17:16-34)

As Paul awaited the arrival of Silas and Timothy from Thessalonica, he had time to observe the flow of life in Athens, which was the intellectual and religious center of Greece. How did Paul choose to spend his time, and why (verses 16-17)?

4. Paul on Mars Hill (Acts 17:21-32)

After Paul preached the gospel in the marketplace he was invited to present his beliefs in the Areopagus, where he preached his most famous sermon. Please read Paul's sermon several times! It is a marvelous insight into the Person and nature of God and His relationship with His creation. Also notice how Paul moved his listeners away from their idols to the truth of Jesus Christ. Briefly outline the following elements of Paul's sermon:

Paul's observation of the Greeks' worship and "The Unknown God" (verses 22-23):

Paul's review of the past (verses 24-29):

Paul's description of the present (verses 27 and 30):

Paul's description of the future (verse 31):

The response God is looking for from all mankind: What does Paul tell the Athenians that God wants them to do (verse 30)?

What were the reactions to Paul's sermon in:

—verse 32?

—verses 33-34?

...and Your Heart's Response

- *Serve behind the scenes.* We don't know much about Jason, the unsung hero in verses 7-9, who seems to have simply provided shelter for the missionary team and vouched for them. But this man's ministry made Paul and Silas's jobs more effective because they didn't have to worry about a place to stay. How does Jason's example encourage you as you serve God and His people? What can you do for others behind the scenes?

- *Search the Scriptures.* The people of Berea opened the Scriptures for themselves and searched for truths to verify or disprove the teachings they heard (verse 11). When you evaluate the sermons you hear, the books you read, and the teachings of individuals, remember the Bereans and follow their example. How are you doing at opening your Bible and digging out the truths that will help you know what you are to believe?

- *Tailor your message to the hearer.* Paul began his sermon to the Athenians by acknowledging their religious interests and practices (verse 22). He first found common ground—and then told his audience about Jesus. What have you learned from Paul's approach that will help you witness to your family, neighbors, workmates, and even strangers who cross your path?

Relying on the Power of the Spirit

What was the result of the Spirit's power and use of Paul and his team? Lives were revolutionized. Social barriers were broken down. Prison doors were opened. The power of the gospel caused people to care deeply for one another and stirred them to worship God.

Your world needs fresh evidence of the power of the Holy Spirit as seen in your life and your message. Ask God for the courage and the wisdom to share the good news of Jesus Christ with the variety of people you meet.

> The Helper, the Holy Spirit, whom the Father will send in My name, He will teach you all things, and bring to your remembrance all things that I said to you (John 14:26).

Lesson 18

Working as a Team

The work of Christ's body, the church, requires a team effort of individuals, each possessing different gifts and abilities. This teamwork—"body life" in action—was seen in the church at Antioch, where Paul and a group of men taught and led the church.

But in Acts 18, Paul was alone. Silas and Timothy were still in Thessalonica. Having left Athens alone, Paul arrived at his next place of ministry, Corinth. Here he encountered an incredible married couple, Priscilla and Aquila. This dynamic duo would become an important part of not only Paul's team, but also teams at several other churches over the course of time.

God's Message...

1. Paul in Corinth (Acts 18:1-17)

   Look at Acts 17:32-34. What does "after these things" refer to in Acts 18:1?

   What do you learn about Aquila and Priscilla from verses 2-3?

   List Paul's activities after arriving in the city of Corinth (verses 4-5).

   What do you learn about Paul's opposition in...

   verse 6?

   verses 12-13?

   What occurred in verses 7-8?

   Outline the Lord's reassurance to Paul in a vision (verses 9-10).

   Do not...

But instead…

Because…

What did Paul do after hearing the message of the Lord (verse 11)?

Summarize what happened in verses 12-17.

2. Paul's return to Antioch (Acts 18:18-22)

Who accompanied Paul when he left Corinth (verse 18)?

What do you also learn about Paul (verse 18)?

Describe Paul's time in Ephesus in relation to Priscilla and Aquila (verses 19).

As you walk through Paul's ministry in Ephesus, what do you see him doing (verse 19)?

What was the response of the people to Paul's presence and teaching, and what was Paul's answer (verse 20)?

Before Paul left Ephesus, what did Paul promise the Jews (verse 21)?

What was Paul's final destination, according to verse 22?

As long as he was in the area, what did Paul decide to do and for what purpose (verse 23)?

3. Apollos in Ephesus (Acts 18:24-28)

List what you learn about Apollos in verses 24-25.

There was one flaw in the knowledge and teaching of this godly Jewish believer—Apollos knew only the baptism of John. How did Aquila and Priscilla meet Apollos (verse 26)?

What did Aquila and Priscilla do, and how did they help Apollos to further understand the gospel message (verse 26)?

How did the believers in Ephesus help Apollos when he decided to go to the region of Achaia (verse 27)?

How did Apollos help the believers in Corinth (verses 27-28)?

...and Your Heart's Response

- *Work as a team.* Aquila and Priscilla provide a terrific role model for God's desire that couples complement each other, not compete with each other. What steps can you and your husband take to become a better complement to each other?

If you are single, read 1 Corinthians 7:32. What does it say about those who are single?

- *Be sensitive to the needs of others.* Acts 18:5 is a good reminder to be sensitive to the spiritual needs of the people around you. Paul was "compelled by the Spirit" (Acts 18:5) to preach Christ to the Jews in Corinth. Who is God's Spirit urging you to speak to? Write down your response. Then follow through.

- *Be a mentor.* Paul was not only a preacher, but a dedicated mentor. He worked with young believers like Timothy and Titus. He trained Priscilla and Aquila and left them behind in Ephesus to disciple new believers. What did Paul write in Titus 2:3-5 about women mentoring women in the church?

Relying on the Power of the Spirit

Do you want to know an easy and effective way for the power of God's Spirit to exhibit itself to the lost? Do as Priscilla and Aquila did—open your home in hospitality. Hospitality creates a great opportunity for you to share about salvation with unbelievers. Married or single, when you open your heart and your home, others will see the reality of God in your life! Who could you invite over? Pray. Look around and act.

I do not pray that You should take them out of the world, but that You should keep them from the evil one...As You sent Me into the world, I also have sent them into the world (John 17:15-16).

Lesson 19

Building Up the Saints

The apostle Paul knew that conforming to the image of Christ would be an ongoing process for the people in the new churches he and his team helped establish. Change would be difficult. That was because, as you have been learning, he and his team had spent precious little time in the different cities where churches were founded—in some cases, only two to three weeks! Paul longed to return to the fledgling churches to further equip them in their spiritual growth. Therefore, he launched his third and final missionary journey to fulfill a promise he made in Acts 18:21.

God's Message...

The beginning of Paul's third missionary journey could be easily overlooked if we don't read what Acts 18:22-23 says.

Read these two verses and list, in order, the places Paul visited after leaving Ephesus the first time.

1. The disciples of John (Acts 19:1-7)

   Beginning at Antioch, Paul journeyed to Ephesus on the west coast of Asia Minor. What two pieces of information were lacking in a group of the disciples of John whom Paul met?

   Verse 2—

   Verse 4—

   What action was taken as a result of their newfound information about the Holy Spirit and the finished work of Christ (verse 5)?

   With what result (verse 6)?

   Besides these disciples of John in Acts 19, list the other two groups who gave testimony to the presence of the Holy Spirit and spoke in tongues.

   Group 1—Acts 2:1-4

   Group 2—Acts 10:44-48

   Group 3—Acts 19:6-7

Just a note: These three outpourings of the Holy Spirit are the only occurrences recorded in the New Testament. These displays were God's way of uniting three groups into the church with the same visible manifestation of His Spirit. In addition, all three experiences occurred with an apostle present—Peter in the first two instances, and Paul in the third.

2. Paul's ministry in Ephesus (19:8-20)

Describe Paul's first three months of ministry (verse 8).

Describe Paul's final two years of ministry (verses 9-12).

How far-reaching was Paul's ministry (verse 10)?

What miracles occurred during his ministry (verses 11-12)?

Who was trying to copy Paul's ministry, and with what results (verses 13-16)?

What effect did a visible testimony of the gospel have among the people (verses 18-19)?

How does the final "progress report" read in verse 20?

3. The riot in Ephesus (19:21-41)

The message of the gospel was producing much fruit. In the midst of this "success," Paul decided to leave Ephesus. What reason did he give for leaving (verse 21)?

As Paul prepared to leave, what did he do to ensure the believers in Macedonia and Achaia were taught and encouraged in the faith (verse 22)?

In verses 23-29, we learn about a riot in Ephesus. In a few words, what was the reason for the riot?

What methods of attack did the instigators and rioters use in...

verses 24-27?

verse 28?

verse 29?

What was Paul's desire (verses 30-31)?

How did the town clerk finally get the rioting crowd to disperse (verses 35-41, see especially verse 40)?

...and Your Heart's Response

- *Keep your promises.* Paul had earlier told the Jews in Ephesus, "I will return again to you, God willing" (Acts 18:21). About one year later, God gave Paul the opportunity to fulfill his promise and revisit the city. Are there any promises you made that you have not fulfilled? Make a note and keep your promises!

- *Build others up.* Paul emphasized two major concerns— evangelizing the lost and edifying the saints. Maybe you can't be as aggressive in evangelism as Paul was, but you can come alongside others and share what you do know. Be someone who builds others up—through acts of kindness, by passing on lessons learned, by being real, by being you. Who can you pour your life into starting this week?

- *Count the cost.* One lesson repeated throughout the book of Acts is that a powerful ministry will always meet powerful opposition. What do these verses say about this possibility?

    2 Timothy 3:12—

    John 15:33—

How does 1 Corinthians 16:13 encourage you?

Relying on the Power of the Spirit

While in Ephesus, for more than two years Paul daily taught the people and evangelized the lost. He just trudged along being faithful where he was, doing whatever he could and whatever was needed one day at a time. What was the result? "All who dwelt in Asia heard the word of the Lord Jesus" (Acts 19:10).

Please don't be discouraged if it seems to you that your ministry is insignificant. It's not. Keep plodding along, working faithfully, and loving others. The cumulative effect of your labors will one day amaze you!

The baptism of the Spirit and the gift of the Spirit are inter-related. The baptism puts me in Christ; the gift puts Christ in me. The one makes me a member of His mystical Body; the other makes my material body the Holy Spirit's Temple.[18]

—John Phillips

Lesson 20

Serving Others

ACTS 20

Do you keep a journal? Maybe the many journals I've kept over the years were the beginning of my writing ministry! I keep journals to record spiritual growth, sermons notes, my travels—even journals for ideas. Well, my friend, the apostle Paul was a keeper of journals, and you and I can thank God that he was, because today, 20-plus centuries later, we can still read the information he recorded from his missionary journeys.

Acts 20 is a record of the conclusion of Paul's third and final missionary journey. On this trip, instead of heading to his home church in Antioch, Paul aimed for Jerusalem, hand-carrying an offering from the churches in Greece and Asia to the church in Jerusalem. Whoever Paul was, he had a heart for serving others.

God's Message...

1. Paul's travels to Corinth (Acts 20:1-4)

   Look back at Acts 19:24-25. What was the "uproar" referred to in Acts 20:1?

   As Paul traveled toward Corinth, what happened, according to 2 Corinthians 7:5-6?

   How long did Paul stay in Greece/Corinth (Acts 20:2-3)?

   Read Acts 20:4-5. List the men who helped gather the contributions for the church in Jerusalem, and the church or region each represented (Acts 20:4-5):

Men's names	Church/area
—	
—	
—	
—	
—	
—	

—

2. Paul's final visit to Troas (Acts 20:5-12)

Where was Paul planning to meet the men who would travel with him to Jerusalem (verse 5)?

Briefly describe the miracle that occurred while Paul was preaching in Troas (verses 7-12).

3. Paul's meeting with the Ephesian elders (Acts 20:13-38)

When Paul arrived in Miletus, he summoned the elders of the church at Ephesus in order to bid them farewell. Their willingness to travel about 35-plus miles to meet with Paul shows their devotion to him. What was Paul's attitude toward his ministry in Ephesus (verses 18-19)?

What more do you learn about Paul's ministry style in verse 27?

What was Paul anticipating as he moved toward Jerusalem, and why (verses 22-23)?

Regardless of what awaited him, what was Paul's purpose (verse 24)?

List some of the warning signs Paul gave to the church leaders from Ephesus (verses 29-31).

What was the essence of Paul's benediction (verse 32)?

How did the church leaders react toward Paul's departure (verses 36-38)?

...and Your Heart's Response

- *Respond positively to God's "No."* In Acts 19:21, Paul's Plan A was to go to Rome, but up to this point God has sovereignly said, "No." What did Paul do? Did he get mad, have a fit, and do his own thing anyway? No, he took God's *no* to his Plan A as a *yes* for a Plan B—for some other way God wanted him to serve. The result? Paul sat down and wrote a letter to the Romans—the book of Romans! God's *no* to Paul's Plan A led to his writing Romans, which is often referred to as "the Gospel of God."

Is there anything you want to do that God is saying *no* to you today? Ask God to give you wisdom to see beyond the *no* to His *yes* for your life today. And don't forget—

God's *no* always has a purpose. Pray to understand, accept, and fulfill that purpose.

- *Work on your spiritual maturity.* Review Paul's speech to the Ephesian church elders in Acts 20:18-21 and note or circle in your Bible the phrases that point to Paul's humility, compassion, endurance, boldness, and honesty. Each of these is a desired mark of maturity for you as a woman. Try this little test: Rate yourself on a scale of 1-5 (5 being perfect) on each of these character qualities. Then note one thing you can—and will—do to improve your score.

  Humility—Rating (   )

  Compassion—Rating (   )

  Endurance—Rating (   )

Relying on the Power of the Spirit

For Paul, serving others was not conditional. He didn't serve only when he felt good or thought the time was right. No, Paul relied on the power of the Spirit to enable him and see him through even the worst!

Are you a "fair-weather servant" who serves only when it's convenient? If so, open your heart to the needs of others. Start with those under your own roof. Sure, there may be a little inconvenience along the way! If so, think of Paul and ask yourself: What would have happened if Paul had ever said, "I'm too busy to serve today"?

~~

The Holy Spirit is God at work.[19]

—D.L. MOODY

Lesson 21

Responding to
the Spirit's Leading

ACTS 21–22

he book of Acts is laced through and through with situations where the Holy Spirit directed, guided, and led the members of the newly formed churches. In the later chapters, beginning with Paul's conversion on the Damascus Road, Paul received guidance and direction from the Holy Spirit. In every case, Paul obeyed—and God blessed. As we make our way through Acts 21 and 22, we see God directing Paul toward a fate that others warned will lead to him being imprisoned. What should Paul do? God's Spirit has not led him astray to this point, but should he listen to what others are saying? Let's see what happens!

God's Message...

1. Paul's journey to Tyre (Acts 21:1-6)

   What warning did the disciples give to Paul on the way to Tyre (verse 4)?

   Looking back, what did Paul say about himself in Acts 20:22?

   What had the Spirit testified would happen to Paul as he ministered in city after city (Acts 20:23)?

2. Paul's journey to Caesarea (Acts 21:7-14)

   Meet Philip...again. Philip (verses 7-8) is in Caesarea, but this is not the first we meet him. To review Philip's back story, look at these verses again and note Philip's ministry and the role of the Holy Spirit.

   Acts 6:1-5—

   Acts 8:5-8—

   Acts 8:26-40—

   Where (verse 26)—

   What (verses 27-38)—

Meet Agabus. Read Acts 21:10-11. How did the prophet Agabus demonstrate what was going to happen to Paul in Jerusalem, according to the Holy Spirit (verse 11)?

How did the disciples respond to Agabus's prophecy (verses 12-13)?

How did Paul respond to the disciples' reaction to Agabus's prophecy (verse 13)?

How did this scene end in verse 14?

3. Paul's arrival in Jerusalem (Acts 21:15-40)

Upon arriving in Jerusalem, who did Paul meet with and what was his report (verses 18-19)?

List the accusations that were made against Paul in verse 21.

—

—

—

Look at Acts 21:23-26. To counter this slander, what did the leaders tell Paul to do in verses 23 and 24 to demonstrate that he did in fact follow the customs of the Jews?

According to verses 25-26, what were the Gentile believers told to do, and how did Paul respond to the instructions he was given by the church leaders?

While Paul was in the temple (verses 26-40), he was maligned and accused by Jews from Asia (verse 27). What did they accuse him of?

Accusation #1 (verse 28)—

Accusation #2 (verses 28-29)—

What occurred after these accusations were made (verses 30-31)?

Briefly describe how Paul was rescued (verses 31-36).

After correcting the Roman commander's case of mistaken identity, what did Paul request (verses 37-40)?

From here onward, you will find the chart below a helpful reference as you follow the key events in Paul's life in Acts 21–28. In the pages ahead, you'll see reminders to look at this chart so you can better understand the chronology of Paul's journey.

Paul the Prisoner... *Ambassador in Chains* Acts 21:18–28:31						
21:18	22:30	23:31	25:1	25:13	26:1	28:31
Before the Mob	Before the Council	Before the Governors		Before the King	Before Jews	
		Felix	Festus	Agrippa		
Jerusalem		Caesarea			Rome	
Accused		Absolved			Awaiting Trial	

4. Paul speaks to an angry mob (Acts 22:1-21)

Describe Paul's life before he met Jesus Christ (verses 1-5).

Describe how Paul met Jesus (verses 6-16).

What happened to Paul after his meeting with Christ (verses 17-21)?

In verses 22-28, Paul revealed he was a Roman citizen, and as such, did not deserve the treatment he had received. What happened immediately, according to verse 29?

What happened the next day (verse 30)?

...and Your Heart's Response

- *Serve others in the church.* In chapter 21, we met Philip, who had four single daughters who each had a ministry (verse 9). What did Paul say is the difference in focus for married women and single women, according to 1 Corinthians 7:34?

  If you are single, what can you do to serve in your local church, to use your spiritual gifts and abilities?

If you are married, how can you encourage and support single women in your congregation toward greater service?

Relying on the Power of the Spirit

The Holy Spirit led and prepared Paul for the moment when he would stand before a large, angry crowd. Yet this was a divine appointment. God was giving him the opportunity to share his testimony, to share Christ with a multitude of people. Your testimony backed up by your life is a powerful tool when lived in reliance upon the power of the Spirit. Make sure you "walk the walk" and prepare your testimony so you are ready to "talk the talk"—and share the truth about Christ.

The Spirit also helps in our weaknesses. For we do not know what we should pray for as we ought, but the Spirit Himself makes intercession for us (Romans 8:26).

Lesson 22

Witnessing the Unfolding Plan of God

ACTS 23

As we come to Acts 23, the apostle Paul has been saved from the grasp of an angry Jewish mob bent on killing him. But the Sanhedrin, the ruling body of Israel, is angry with him as well. They too want to kill him. In the midst of all this turmoil, the Lord spoke to Paul and assured him that he would bear witness to Him in Rome (verse 11).

Your crisis situations might not be as unnerving and life-threatening as Paul's were, but as with Paul, God has a plan for you. If you keep your eyes on Jesus, rely on the Holy Spirit, and patiently wait for God to unfold His plan, you will reap great blessings on the other side.

God's Message...

1. Paul before the Sanhedrin (Acts 22:30–23:11)

    Fresh from being saved from the mob the day before, Paul is now brought before the nation's Jewish ruling body—the Sanhedrin—to give testimony (see the chart on page 130). This is the fifth time the Sanhedrin has been put in a position to evaluate the claims of Christ.

    Sensing he was not going to have a chance to bear witness to Christ and knowing the makeup of the ruling body, what did Paul declare in Acts 23:6?

    What were the results of Paul's statement, and why (verses 7-10)?

    How did God encourage and confirm Paul's decision to travel to Jerusalem (verse 11)?

2. The plot to kill Paul (Acts 23:12-22)

    The next day, after God pledged to deliver Paul safely to Rome, what happened (verses 12-13)?

How did the assassins plan to carry out their scheme, and with whose assistance (verses 14-15)?

What seeming "coincidence" alerted Paul to the plan to kill him (verse 16)?

How were Paul's nephew's observations communicated to the Romans (verses 17-22)?

3. Paul is sent to Caesarea (Acts 23:23-35)

How did the Romans respond to Paul's nephew's information (verses 23-24)?

Jot down what happened next (verses 25-35):

A letter was sent by whom (verse 26)?

The letter was sent to whom (verse 26)?

What information did the letter contain (verses 27-30)?

How quickly did the soldiers leave with Paul and the letter (verse 31)?

What was Felix's response to the letter (verses 33-35)?

...and Your Heart's Response

- *Give a word of encouragement.* Read the verses below and describe how God encouraged Paul up to this point in his ministry.

    Acts 16:9—

    Acts 18:9-10—

    Acts 22:17—

    Acts 23:11—

    Today, God uses His Word, His Spirit, and His people to encourage one another when they are lonely and discouraged. Who can you encourage? List a few names of people who come to mind, and ask God how you can encourage them.

- *Train your children to serve.* If you have children, don't assume they are too young to do much for the Lord. What are some ways you can begin to involve your children in the ministries at your church?

Relying on the Power of the Spirit

The apostle Paul stated, "I have lived in all good conscience before God until this day" (Acts 23:1). Obedience to the will of God was why Paul experienced the power of the Holy Spirit. When you are obedient to God's will, you can expect some of the same divine benefits Paul experienced. For instance:

> *God's presence* (verse 11). You can count on God to stand by you just as He stood by Paul.
>
> *God's protection* (verses 12-32). God preserves and protects His children for the work at hand.
>
> *God's placement* (verses 33-35). As you are obedient and rely on the Holy Spirit, God will place you where He wants you.

When you do things God's way—in the Spirit—you will do the right things, in the right way, at the right time, with the right motives.

My grace is sufficient for you, for My strength is made perfect in weakness (2 Corinthians 12:9).

Lesson 23

Fulfilling Your Purpose

ACTS 24

*H*ave you thought much about God's purpose for you—why you are alive and what God wants you to do with your life? I have to admit that the launching point of my obsession with discovering and attempting to fulfill God's purposes for me was when I read Acts 13 for the very first time as a believer—at age 28—when my life was already one-third over!

We have already been through Acts 13 in this Bible study, but I want you to think about this statement made by Paul about King David: "David, after he had served his own generation by the will of God, fell asleep" (verse 36). Clearly God had a purpose for David. And, my friend, He has a purpose for you and me. Now read on to see how God is propelling Paul toward His purpose.

God's Message...

1. Paul's purpose (Acts 9:1-16)

   During his first encounter with the risen Lord, Paul was given his "marching orders," his purpose. Read Acts 9:1-16 to review Paul's conversion from being a persecutor of Christians to becoming a Christian himself. What did God tell Ananias about Paul's future and purpose in...

   verse 15?

   verse 16?

2. Paul's defense before Felix (Acts 24:1-21)

   Quickly review Acts 23:31-35. Paul's case was bounced back and forth and then put on hold. According to Acts 24:1, what happened five days after Paul was held in Herod's judgment hall?

   The lies proffered by the prosecution (verses 1-9)

   What three accusations were brought against Paul?

   Charge #1 (verses 1-5a)—

   Charge #2 (verse 5b)—

   Charge #3 (verses 6-9)—

   Paul's defense against the accusations (verses 10-21)

Just as 1 Peter 3:15 instructs, Paul was "ready to give a defense to everyone who asks you a reason for the hope that is in you." What was Paul's attitude as he began his defense in Acts 24:10?

What was Paul's response to Charge #1 (verses 10-13)?

To Charge #2 (verses 14,21)?

To Charge #3 (verses 15-20)?

3. The decisions of Felix, the governor (Acts 24:22-27)

What was Felix's initial response to Paul's defense in verse 22?

What arrangements were made for Paul in verse 23?

Describe the relationship Felix and his wife, Drusilla, developed with Paul (verses 24-26).

What do you learn about the next two years of Paul's life from verses 26 and 27?

...and Your Heart's Response

- *Test what you hear.* Tertullus was a lawyer trained to sound eloquent and convincing. Yet he was not fair or truthful. Test everything you hear. Search the Scriptures so you know God's truth. What overarching truth is taught in Ephesians 4:29 regarding your speech?

- *Eliminate flattery.* The lawyer Tertullus flattered the governor, Felix, and manipulated the people. What is the overarching truth in Ephesians 4:15 regarding your heart and your speech?

Relying on the Power of the Spirit

Whether you realize it or not, your purpose is even clearer than Paul's was. You will have to dig a little for the specifics, but your purposes are fully revealed right in your Bible.

Are you a believer? If so, your purpose is clear!
Are you a wife? If so, your purpose is clear!
Are you a mother? If so, your purpose is clear!
Are you a woman? If so, your purpose is clear!
Are you a part of a church? If so, your purpose is clear!

Read God's Word and find out what God wants you to be doing with your life. Be obedient to do what you are learning—and rely on the Spirit to work in and through you!

> *Reliance on the Spirit is not intended to foster an attitude of "I can't do it," but one of "I can do this through Him who strengthens me" (Philippians 4:13). The Christian should never complain of want of ability and power. If we sin, it is because we choose to sin, not because we lack the ability to say no to temptation.*[20]

—JERRY BRIDGES

Dealing with Waiting

ACTS 25–26

How long can you wait?

You might say, "It depends on what I'm waiting for." Well, Sarah, the wife of Abraham, was told she would bear a son. Little did she know she would have to wait 25 years for that child. How did Sarah deal with waiting? Not so well! In fact she decided to take matters into her own hands and offered her servant Hagar to Abraham so Hagar would bear the promised son.

Unfortunately, Ishmael wasn't the son God promised, and the world is living with the consequences of Sarah's lack of patience.

Paul too was promised something he greatly wanted. He was told by God that he would go to Rome. But due to the political climate, he was still stuck in Caesarea two years after arriving there. Let's see how Paul dealt with waiting.

God's Message...

1. Festus and Paul (Acts 25:1-12)

   After Paul waited two years for a new governor to hear his case and grant him freedom, Festus arrived in Caesarea...and left three days later without judging Paul's case (see the chart on page 130). Where did Festus travel to after leaving Caesarea (verse 1), and with whom did he meet (verse 2)?

   What was the main item on this group's agenda (verse 2)?

   What did the Jewish leaders request, and what was their motive (verse 3)?

   When Festus spoke, what was his decision before he returned to Caesarea (verses 4-5)?

   Once Paul's hearing reconvened in Caesarea, many false accusations were made against him (verses 6-7). What was Festus's final suggestion (verse 9)?

   How did Paul respond to Festus's request (verses 10-12)?

2. Festus and Agrippa (Acts 25:13-22)

   In these verses, Festus is bringing Agrippa, a visiting monarch, up to date on the progression of Paul's case.

How did Festus respond to Paul's case and his appeal to go to Rome (verses 20-21)?

How did Agrippa respond after hearing about the history of Paul's case (verse 22)?

3. Paul before Agrippa (Acts 25:23–26:32)

When Festus introduced Paul to Agrippa, what did he say about Paul in…

verse 24?

verse 25?

What was Festus hoping would be accomplished in the meeting with Agrippa (verses 26-27)?

Finally, Paul was allowed to speak (Acts 26:1—again, see the chart on page 130). Be sure to read his exciting testimony. He chose to share about his religious upbringing and training, and his zeal in persecuting followers of Jesus of Nazareth (verses 2-11). Paul then went on to describe his encounter with Jesus on the road to Damascus (verses 12-18) and the changes that occurred in his life afterward (verses 19-23).

Anytime Christians share their testimony, they can expect a variety of responses. Read verses 23-32, and note the responses of…

Festus (verse 24)—

King Agrippa (verse 28)—

What was the verdict reached by Festus and Agrippa and their group (verse 31)?

What other conclusion was agreed on (verse 32)?

...and Your Heart's Response

- *Keep a positive perspective.* Imagine standing up to speak to a group of military officers, prominent rulers, and influential people who are hostile toward you. Would you see this setting as a crisis or an opportunity? Paul saw his audience in Caesarea as another opportunity to share his testimony.

  How does Paul's example and positive perspective encourage your view of your life situation?

- *Share a changed life.* In his longest speech in the book of Acts—28 verses!—Paul reviewed his past. The power of his testimony lay in the abrupt changes that took place in his life once he met Jesus. As an exercise in joy, list some of the positive changes that have taken place in you since you became a Christian. Then give thanks to God for His work in transforming you into the image of His Son (Romans 8:29).

Relying on the Power of the Spirit

How is your patience quotient right about now? Do you ever feel like Sarah did? That you have been praying for some concern and nothing seems to be happening? And Paul? Surely he wondered about God's promise that he would go to Rome. Well, Sarah did get her son, and as you will see in Acts 28:16, Paul did make it to Rome. In both cases, prayers were answered and God's promises were kept—in God's timing.

Are there prayers you regularly lift to the Lord that are still unanswered? Be patient. God has a plan—and a purpose. Pray for the patience only the Holy Spirit can give you while you wait. Pray to be content right where you are, with what you have and don't have, in whatever circumstance. Take to heart the encouragement of the psalmist:

I waited patiently for the LORD;
and He inclined to me,
and heard my cry (Psalm 40:1).

Lesson 25

Standing on the Promises of God

ACTS 27–28

*I*n Acts 1:8, God promised power—and we have witnessed that power on display from the steps of the temple in Jerusalem to the steps of the Areopagus in Athens and now finally to the interlocking stones of the Appian Way as they point toward Rome.

Jesus promised Paul that he would "bear [His] name before Gentiles, kings, and the children of Israel" (Acts 9:15). For Paul, the journey was just about over (see the chart on page 130). For you and me, the promise of God's power for our journey is far from over!

God's Message...

1. Paul's journey to Rome (Acts 27:1–28:1-10)

Phase one: From Caesarea to Sidon (Acts 27:1-3)

To review, what did Agrippa say in Acts 26:32 before Festus ordered Paul sent to Rome?

Luke specifically listed himself (note his use of the pronoun "we") and two others. Who was with Luke in Acts 27:1-2, and what is said about them?

—

—

What comments did Luke have about Julius (verse 3)?

Phase two: From Sidon to Myra (Acts 27:4-7)

Describe the progress of their journey (verses 6-7).

Phase three: From Myra to Fair Havens (Acts 27:8-12)

What warning did Paul give (verses 9-10)?

Why didn't the fellow passengers heed Paul's warning (verse 12)?

Phase four: From Fair Havens to Malta (Acts 27:13-44)

Give a few details about the severity of the storm and its duration (verses 13-19).

Due to the magnitude of the storm, what was the prevailing attitude of the people on the ship (verse 20)?

What three things did Paul tell the disheartened people?

The negative (verse 21)—

The positive (verse 22)—

The reason for Paul's optimism (verses 23-26)—

Describe the ship's arrival at Malta (verses 27-44):

How close did the ship get to land?

What were the plans of the sailors?

Who stopped the soldiers' plans?

What was Paul's prediction in verse 22, and what happened (verse 44)?

Phase five: Malta and on to Rome (Acts 28:1-11)

Give some of the details of the shipwrecked passengers' stay in Malta:

The locals—

The locals' final impression of Paul—

Publius's hospitality—

Publius's father—

Paul's ministry—

The length of their stay in Malta—

2. Paul's journey and imprisonment in Rome (Acts 28:12-30)

List the three brief stops Paul and his companions made before meeting the brethren near Rome (verses 12-14).

—

—

—

Describe Paul's living conditions in Rome (verse 16).

In a few words, state the purpose of the two meetings Paul scheduled with the Jewish leaders in Rome.

—Meeting #1 (verses 17-22):

—Meeting #2 (verses 23-29):

How did Paul spend the next two years in Rome (verses 30-31)?

...and Your Heart's Response

- *Encourage others.* God offered timely words of encouragement to Paul during the darkest hour of the storm, and today, God encourages you and me through our storms. To keep from becoming discouraged, read your Bible, pray, walk by the Spirit, and be part of a vibrant church fellowship. Then look around and ask: Who needs encouragement today?

- *Serve others.* The apostle Paul is considered as one of the giants of the Christian faith. Today we owe Paul a great debt for his leadership, vision, and never-ending pursuit of God's purpose, as well as the 13 books of the New Testament he penned. Look again at Acts 28:2-3. What do you see the apostle Paul doing soon after the shipwreck on Malta?

In Matthew 23:11, what did Jesus say is a mark of greatness?

Jesus came to serve others. Paul too was a servant. And now it's your turn. List a few of the people God is asking you to serve, starting with your family. Pray for them, and then, like Jesus, serve them (Matthew 20:28)!

- *Make the most of negative situations.* Paul spent four years as a prisoner and used these "down times" as opportunities to teach, preach, counsel, and write.[21]

With Paul as your example, determine to turn your negatives into positives by finding ways to do something useful. There is never a time or place in which you cannot glorify God and serve Him and others. What will your first step forward be?

Relying on the Power of the Spirit

As we close the book of Acts, it has been 30 years since Jesus gave His final command to a small band of Christians just before He returned to heaven (Acts 1). He told them to take His message of salvation to the ends of the earth. And when God commands, He also supplies the needed resources. Jesus said, "You shall receive power when the Holy Spirit has come upon you" (Acts 1:8).

Today God's message is the same, and the power of the Holy Spirit is the same. As you rely on the Spirit, He will empower you in your ministry to your family and the family of God. Walk by the Spirit and pass on the truth of the gospel first to your family, and then others.

> *God is not far off. In the Holy Spirit, the Triune God comes close, so close as to actually enter into each believer. He is even more intimate with us now than in the incarnation. Through the operation of the Spirit he has truly become Immanuel, "God with us."*[22]
>
> —Millard Erickson

Notes

1. Taken from Elizabeth George, *A Woman After God's Own Heart* (Eugene, OR: Harvest House, 2006), pp. 31-36.

2. Mal Couch, gen. ed., *A Bible Handbook to the Acts of the Apostles* (Grand Rapids: Kregel, 1999), p. 128.

3. David Wilkerson, *The Cross and the Switchblade* (Grand Rapids: Chosen Books, 2008), pp. 52-53.

4. J.A. Alexander, *Commentary on the Acts of the Apostles* (Grand Rapids: Zondervan, 1956), p. 113.

5. Being filled with the Holy Spirit "indicates a state or condition of fullness in respect to the control of the Holy Spirit over a person's life. It denotes not a method toward spiritual maturity or Spirit control but the condition of spiritual maturity or Spirit control." Couch, gen. ed., *A Bible Handbook to the Acts of the Apostles,* p. 63.

6. Henry Blackaby, Mel Blackaby, *Experiencing the Holy Spirit* (Colorado Springs: Multnomah, 2009), page unknown.

7. Couch, gen. ed., *A Bible Handbook to the Acts of the Apostles,* p. 126.

8. Steve Childers, quote found online but source unknown.

9. Blackaby, Blackaby, *Experiencing the Holy Spirit*, page unknown.

10. Jerry Bridges, *The Pursuit of Holiness* (Colorado Springs: NavPress, 1978), page unknown.

11. John Phillips, *Exploring Acts* (Grand Rapids: Kregel, 1986), p. 210.

12. Richard Halverson, as cited in Albert M. Wells Jr., *Inspiring Quotations—Contemporary & Classical* (Nashville: Thomas Nelson, 1988), p. 89.

13. Phillips, *Exploring Acts*, p. 220.

14. Phillips, *Exploring Acts*, p. 301.

15. John MacArthur, *The MacArthur Daily Bible* (Nashville: Thomas Nelson, 2003), p. 997.

16. Millard J. Erickson, *Christian Theology* (Grand Rapids; Baker Book House, 1985), p. 883.

17. Erwin and Rebecca Lutzer, *Life-Changing Bible Verses You Should Know* (Eugene, OR: Harvest House, 2011), p.87.

18. Phillips, *Exploring Acts*, p. 377.

19. D.L. Moody, as quoted in Eleanor L. Doan, *The Speakers's Sourcebook* (Grand Rapids: Zondervan, 1977), p. 125.

20. Bridges, *The Pursuit of Holiness*, p. 84. See Luke 22:66-67; Acts 4:5-22; 5:21-40;6:12–7:60; 22;30–23:11.

21. While imprisioned in Rome for two years, Paul wrote Ephesians, Philippians, Colossians, and Philemon.

22. Erickson, *Christian Theology*, p. 863.

BIBLE STUDIES *for* BUSY WOMEN

Character Studies

Old Testament Studies

New Testament Studies

A WOMAN AFTER GOD'S OWN HEART® BIBLE STUDIES

*E*lizabeth takes women step-by-step through the Scriptures, sharing wisdom she's gleaned from more than 30 years as a women's Bible teacher.

Books by Elizabeth George

- Beautiful in God's Eyes
- Beautiful in God's Eyes for Young Women
- Breaking the Worry Habit…Forever
- Finding God's Path Through Your Trials
- Following God with All Your Heart
- The Heart of a Woman Who Prays
- Life Management for Busy Women
- Loving God with All Your Mind
- Loving God with All Your Mind DVD and Workbook
- A Mom After God's Own Heart
- A Mom After God's Own Heart Devotional
- Moments of Grace for a Woman's Heart
- One-Minute Inspirations for Women
- Prayers to Calm Your Heart
- Quiet Confidence for a Woman's Heart
- Raising a Daughter After God's Own Heart
- The Remarkable Women of the Bible
- Small Changes for a Better Life
- Walking with the Women of the Bible
- A Wife After God's Own Heart
- A Woman After God's Own Heart®
- A Woman After God's Own Heart®— Daily Devotional
- A Woman's Daily Walk with God
- A Woman's Guide to Making Right Choices
- A Woman's High Calling
- A Woman's Walk with God
- A Woman Who Reflects the Heart of Jesus
- A Young Woman After God's Own Heart
- A Young Woman After God's Own Heart— A Devotional
- A Young Woman's Guide to Discovering Her Bible
- A Young Woman's Guide to Making Right Choices
- A Young Woman's Guide to Prayer
- A Young Woman Who Reflects the Heart of Jesus

Study Guides

- Beautiful in God's Eyes Growth & Study Guide
- Finding God's Path Through Your Trials Growth & Study Guide
- Following God with All Your Heart Growth & Study Guide
- Life Management for Busy Women Growth & Study Guide
- Loving God with All Your Mind Growth & Study Guide
- Loving God with All Your Mind Interactive Workbook
- A Mom After God's Own Heart Growth & Study Guide
- The Remarkable Women of the Bible Growth & Study Guide
- Small Changes for a Better Life Growth & Study Guide
- A Wife After God's Own Heart Growth & Study Guide
- A Woman After God's Own Heart® Growth & Study Guide
- A Woman Who Reflects the Heart of Jesus Growth & Study Guide

Children's Books

- A Girl After God's Own Heart
- A Girl After God's Own Heart Devotional
- A Girl's Guide to Making Really Good Choices
- A Girl's Guide to Discovering Her Bible
- God's Wisdom for Little Girls
- A Little Girl After God's Own Heart

Books by Jim George

- 10 Minutes to Knowing the Men and Women of the Bible
- The Bare Bones Bible® Handbook
- The Bare Bones Bible® Handbook for Teens
- A Boy After God's Own Heart
- A Boy's Guide to Discovering His Bible
- A Boy's Guide to Making Really Good Choices
- A Dad After God's Own Heart
- A Husband After God's Own Heart
- Know Your Bible from A to Z
- A Leader After God's Own Heart
- A Man After God's Own Heart
- A Man After God's Own Heart Devotional
- The Man Who Makes a Difference
- One-Minute Insights for Men
- A Young Man After God's Own Heart
- A Young Man's Guide to Discovering His Bible
- A Young Man's Guide to Making Right Choices

Books by Jim & Elizabeth George

- A Couple After God's Own Heart
- A Couple After God's Own Heart Interactive Workbook
- God's Wisdom for Little Boys
- A Little Boy After God's Own Heart

About the Author

Elizabeth George is a bestselling author and speaker whose passion is to teach the Bible in a way that changes women's lives. For information about Elizabeth's books or speaking ministry, to sign up for her mailings, or to share how God has used this book in your life, please contact Elizabeth at:

www.ElizabethGeorge.com